AF303065

Wodehouse Shaw Chekhov Dante Swift Doré Newton Pushkin Alcott Benedict da Richter Irving Chambers Voltaire Cervantes Shakespeare Bunner Cooke Burton Hale James Hastings Poe Aristotle Hesse Harte Wells Descartes London Andersen Scott Plato Dickens Stevenson Jowett Freud Kant Lawrence Zola Potter Twain Wain Whitman Thoreau Widger Darwin Homer Gogol Tolstoy Toqueville Curtis Busch Vinci Verne Burroughs Crane Vatsyayana Stockton Balzac Turgenev Flaubert Dumas Leslie Hall Willis Doyle Nietzsche Henry Baum Smith Kipling Cotton Kafka Dostoyevsky Goethe Hawthorne Fitzgerald Einstein Garnett Grimm Schiller Engels Maupassant Byron Wilde Molière Machiavelli Montaigne Christie Carroll Stoker Hugo Emerson Cooper Chesterton Haggard Marx Hardy Melville Abbott Defoe Eliot Austen Joyce

tredition®

tredition was established in 2006 by Sandra Latusseck and Soenke Schulz. Based in Hamburg, Germany, tredition offers publishing solutions to authors and publishing houses, combined with worldwide distribution of printed and digital book content. tredition is uniquely positioned to enable authors and publishing houses to create books on their own terms and without conventional manufacturing risks.

For more information please visit: www.tredition.com

TREDITION CLASSICS

This book is part of the TREDITION CLASSICS series. The creators of this series are united by passion for literature and driven by the intention of making all public domain books available in printed format again - worldwide. Most TREDITION CLASSICS titles have been out of print and off the bookstore shelves for decades. At tredition we believe that a great book never goes out of style and that its value is eternal. Several mostly non-profit literature projects provide content to tredition. To support their good work, tredition donates a portion of the proceeds from each sold copy. As a reader of a TREDITION CLASSICS book, you support our mission to save many of the amazing works of world literature from oblivion. See all available books at www.tredition.com.

Project Gutenberg

The content for this book has been graciously provided by Project Gutenberg. Project Gutenberg is a non-profit organization founded by Michael Hart in 1971 at the University of Illinois. The mission of Project Gutenberg is simple: To encourage the creation and distribution of eBooks. Project Gutenberg is the first and largest collection of public domain eBooks.

East Anglia Personal Recollections and Historical Associations

J. Ewing (James Ewing) Ritchie

Imprint

This book is part of TREDITION CLASSICS

Author: J. Ewing (James Ewing) Ritchie
Cover design: Buchgut, Berlin – Germany

Publisher: tredition GmbH, Hamburg - Germany
ISBN: 978-3-8472-2020-6

www.tredition.com
www.tredition.de

PRESS NOTICES OF THE FIRST EDITION.

'We cordially recommend Mr. Ritchie's book to all who wish to pass an agreeable hour and to learn something of the outward actions and inner life of their predecessors. It is full of sketches of East Anglian celebrities, happily touched if lightly limned.' — *East Anglian Daily Times.*

'A very entertaining and enjoyable book. Local gossip, a wide range of reading and industrious research, have enabled the author to enliven his pages with a wide diversity of subjects, specially attractive to East Anglians, but also of much general interest.' — *Daily Chronicle.*

'The work is written in a light gossipy style, and by reason both of it and of the variety of persons introduced is interesting. To a Suffolk or Norfolk man it is, of course, especially attractive. The reader will go through these pages without being wearied by application. They form a pleasant and entertaining contribution to county literature, and "East Anglia" will, we should think, find its way to many of the east country bookshelves.' — *Suffolk Chronicle.*

'The book is as readable and attractive a volume of local chronicles as could be desired. Though all of our readers may not see "eye to eye" with Mr. Ritchie, in regard to political and theological questions, they cannot fail to gain much enjoyment from his excellent delineation of old days in East Anglia.' — *Norwich Mercury.*

'"East Anglia" has the merit of not being a compilation, which is more than can be said of the great majority of books produced in these days to satisfy the revived taste for topographical gossip. Mr. Ritchie is a Suffolk man — the son of a Nonconformist minister of Wrentham in that county — and he looks back to the old neighbourhood and the old times with an affection which is likely to communicate itself to its readers. Altogether we can with confidence recommend this book not only to East Anglians, but to all readers who have any affinity for works of its class.' — *Daily News.*

'Mr. Ritchie's book belongs to a class of which we have none too many, for when well done they illustrate contemporary history in a really charming manner. What with their past grandeur, their present progress, their martyrs, patriots, and authors, there is plenty to tell concerning Eastern counties: and one who writes with native enthusiasm is sure to command an audience.' — *Baptist.*

'Mr. Ritchie, known to the numerous readers of the *Christian World* as "Christopher Crayon," has the pen of a ready, racy, refreshing writer. He never writes a dull line, and never for a moment allows our interest to flag. In the work before us, which is not his first, he is, I should think, at his best. The volume is the outcome of extensive reading, many rambles over the districts described, and of thoughtful observation. We seem to live and move and have our being in East Anglia. Its folk-lore, its traditions, its worthies, its memorable events, are all vividly and charmingly placed before us, and we close the book sorry that there is no more of it, and wondering why it is that works of a similar kind have not more frequently appeared.' — *Northern Pioneer.*

'It has yielded us more gratification than any work that we have read for a considerable time. The book ought to have a wide circulation in the Eastern counties, and will not fail to yield profit and delight wherever it finds its way.' — *Essex Telegraph.*

'Mr. Ritchie has here written a most attractive chapter of autobiography. He recalls the scenes of his early days, and whatever was quaint or striking in connection with them, and finds in his recollections ready pegs on which to hang historical incident and antiquarian curiosities of many kinds. He passes from point to point in a delightfully cheerful and contagious mood. Mr. Ritchie's reading has been as extensive and careful as his observation is keen and his temper genial; and his pages, which appeared in *The Christian World Magazine*, well deserve the honour of book-form, with the additions he has been able to make to them.' — *British Quarterly Review*.

EAST ANGLIA.

PERSONAL RECOLLECTIONS
and
HISTORICAL ASSOCIATIONS.
by
J. EWING RITCHIE.

'Behold, there came wise men from the East to Jerusalem.'

Matthew.

SECOND EDITION,
revised, corrected, and enlarged.
LONDON:
JARROLD & SONS, PATERNOSTER BUILDINGS, E.C.
1893.

p. vPREFACE TO THE SECOND EDITION.

The chapters of which this little work consists originally appeared in the *Christian World Magazine*, where they were so fortunate as to attract favourable notice, and from which they are now reprinted, with a few slight additions, by permission of the Editor. In bringing out a second edition, I have incorporated the substance of other articles originally written for local journals. It is to be hoped, touching as they do a theme not easily exhausted, but always interesting to East Anglians, that they may help to sustain that love of one's county which, alas! like the love of country, is a matter reckoned to be of little importance in these cosmopolitan days, but which, nevertheless, has had not a little share in the formation of that national greatness and glory in which at all times Englishmen believe.

p. viOne word more. I have retained some strictures on the clergy of East Anglia, partly because they were true at the time to which I refer, and partly because it gives me pleasure to own that they are not so now. The Church of England clergyman of to-day is an immense improvement on that of my youth. In ability, in devotion to the duties of his calling, in intelligence, in self-denial, in zeal, he is equal to the clergy of any other denomination. If he has lost his hold upon Hodge, that, at any rate, is not his fault.

Clacton-on-Sea,
January, 1893.

p. 1CHAPTER I.
a suffolk village.

Distinguished people born there—Its Puritans and Nonconformists—The country round Covehithe—Southwold—Suffolk dialect—The Great Eastern Railway.

In his published Memoirs, the great Metternich observes that if he had never been born he never could have loved or hated. Following so illustrious a precedent, I may observe that if I had not been born in East Anglia I never could have been an East Anglian. Whether I should have been wiser or better off had I been born elsewhere, is an interesting question, which, however, it is to be hoped the public will forgive me if I decline to discuss on the present occasion.

In a paper bearing the date of 1667, a Samuel Baker, of Wattisfield Hall, writes: 'I was born at p. 2a village called Wrentham, which place I cannot pass by the mention of without saying thus much, that religion has there flourished longer, and that in much piety; the Gospel and grace of it have been more powerfully and clearly preached, and more generally received; the professors of it have been more sound in the matter and open and steadfast in the profession of it in an hour of temptation, have manifested a greater oneness amongst themselves and have been more eminently preserved from enemies without (albeit they dwell where Satan's seat is encompassed with his malice and rage), than I think in any village of the like capacity in England; which I speak as my duty to the place, but to my particular shame rather than otherwise, that such a dry and barren plant should spring out of such a soil.' I resemble this worthy Mr. Baker in two respects. In the first place, I was born at Wrentham, though at a considerably later period of time than 1667; and, secondly, if he was a barren plant—he of whom we read, in Harmer's Miscellaneous Works, that 'he was a gentleman of fortune and education, very zealous for the Congregational plan of church government and discipline, and a sufferer in its bonds for a good conscience'—what am I?

p. 3Nor was it only piety that existed in this distant parish. If the reader turns to the diary of John Evelyn, under the date of 1679, he will find mention made of a child brought up to London, 'son of one Mr. Wotton, formerly amanuensis to Dr. Andrews, Bishop of Winton, who both read and perfectly understood Hebrew, Greek, Latin, Arabic and Syriac, and most of the modern languages, disputed in divinity, law and all the sciences, was skilful in history, both ecclesiastical and profane; in a word, so universally and solidly learned at eleven years of age that he was looked on as a miracle. Dr. Lloyd, one of the most deep-learned divines of this nation in all sorts of literature, with Dr. Burnet, who had severely examined him, came away astonished, and told me they did not believe there had the like appeared in the world. He had only been instructed by his father, who being himself a learned person, confessed that his son knew all that he himself knew. But what was more admirable than his vast memory was his judgment and invention, he being tried with divers hard questions which required maturity of thought and experience. He was also dexterous in chronology, antiquities, mathematics. In sum, an *intellectus universalis* beyond all that we p. 4reade of Picus Mirandula, and other precoce witts, and yet withal a very humble child.' This prodigy was the son of the Rev. Henry Wotton, minister of Wrentham, Suffolk. Sir William Skippon, a parishioner, in a letter yet extant, describes the wonderful achievements of the little fellow when but five years old. He was admitted at Katherine Hall, Cambridge, some months before he was ten years old. In after-years he was the friend and defender of Bentley and the antagonist of Sir William Temple in the great controversy about ancient and modern learning. He died in 1726, and was buried at Buxted, in Sussex. It is clear that there was no such intellectual phenomenon in all London under the Stuarts as that little Wrentham lad.

Of that village, when I came into the world, my father was the honoured, laborious and successful minister. The meeting-house, as it was called, which stood in the lane leading from the church to the highroad, was a square red brick building, vastly superior to any of the ancient meeting-houses round. It stood in an enclosure, one side of which was devoted to the reception of the farmers' gigs, which, on a Sunday afternoon, when the principal service was held, made quite a respectable show when drawn up in a line. By p. 5the side of it was a cottage, in which lived the woman who kept the place tidy, and her husband, who looked after the horses as they were unharnessed and put in the stable close by. The backs of the gigs were sheltered from the road by a hedge of lilacs, and over the gateway a gigantic elm kept watch and ward. The house in which we lived was also part of the chapel estate, and, if it was a little way off, it was, at any rate, adapted to the wants of a family of quiet habits and simple tastes. On one side of the house was a water-butt, and I can well remember my first sad experience of the wickedness of the world when, getting up one morning to look after my rabbits and other live stock, I found that water-butt had gone, and that there were thieves in a village so rural and renowned for piety as ours. I say renowned, and not without reason. Years and years back there was a pious clergyman of the name of Steffe, who had a son in Dr. Doddridge's Academy, at Daventry, and it is a fact that the great Doctor himself, at some time or other, had been a guest in the village.

In 1741 the Doctor thus records his East Anglian recollections, in a letter to his wife: 'You have great reason to confide in that very kind Providence which has hitherto watched over p. 6us, and has, since the date of my last, brought us about sixty miles nearer London. From Yarmouth we went on Friday morning to Wrentham, where good Mrs. Steffe lives, and from thence to a gentleman's seat, near Walpole, where I was most respectfully entertained. As I had twenty miles to ride yesterday morning, he, though I had never seen him before last Tuesday, brought me almost half-way in his chaise, to make the journey easier. I reached Woodbridge before two, and rode better in the cool of the evening, and had the happiness to be entertained in a very elegant and friendly family, though perfectly a stranger; and, indeed, I have been escorted from one place to another in every mile of my journey by one, and sometimes by two or three, of my brethren in a most respectful and agreeable manner.' Dr. Doddridge's East Anglian recollections seem to have been uncommonly agreeable, owing quite as much, I must candidly confess, to the presence of the sisters as of the brethren. Writing to his wife an account of a little trip on the river, he adds: 'It was a very pleasant day, and I concluded it in the company of one of the finest women I ever beheld, who, though she had seven children grown up to marriageable years, or very near it, is p. 7still herself almost a beauty, and a person of sense, good breeding, and piety, which might astonish one who had not the happiness of being intimately acquainted with you.' What a sly rogue was Dr. Doddridge! How could any wife be jealous when her husband finishes off with such a compliment to herself?

But to return to the good Mrs. Steffe, of whom I am, on my mother's side, a descendant. I must add that as there were great men before Agamemnon, so there were good people in the little village of Wrentham before Mrs. Steffe appeared upon the scene. The Brewsters, who were an ancient family, which seems to have culminated under the glorious usurpation of Oliver Cromwell, were eminently good people in Dr. Doddridge's acceptation of the term, and I fancy did much as lords of the manor—and as inhabitants of Wrentham Hall, a building which had ceased to exist long before my time—to leaven with their goodness the surrounding lump. It seems to me that these Brewsters must have been more or less connected with Brewster the elder—of Robinson's Church at Leyden, who, we are told, came of a wealthy and distinguished family—who was well trained at Cambridge, and, says the historian, 'thence, being first seasoned with p. 8the seeds of grace and virtue, he went to the Court, and there served that religious and godly Mr. Davison divers years, when he was Secretary of State, who found him so discreet and faithful as he trusted him, above all others that were about him, and only employed him in matters of great trust and secrecy; he esteemed him rather as a son than a servant, and for his wisdom and godliness in private, he would converse with him more like a familiar than a master.' When evil times came, this Brewster was living in the big Manor House at Scrooby, and how he and his godly associates were driven into exile by a foolish King and cruel priests is known, or ought to be known, to everyone. Of these Wrentham Brewsters, one served his country in Parliament, or I am very much mistaken. It was to their credit that they sought out godly men, to whom they might entrust the cure of souls. In this respect, when I was a lad, their example certainly had not been followed, and Dissent flourished mainly because the moral instincts of the villagers and farmers and small tradesmen were shocked by hearing men on the Sunday reading the Lessons of the Church, leading the devotions of the people, and preaching sermons, who on the week-days got drunk and led immoral p. 9lives. As to the right of the

State to interfere in matters of religion, as to the danger to religion itself from the establishment of a State Church, as to the liberty of unlicensed prophesying, such topics the simple villagers ignored. All that they felt was that there came to them more of a quickening of the spiritual life, a fuller realization of God and things divine, in the meeting-house than in the parish church. They were not what pious Churchmen so much dread nowadays—Political Dissenters; how could they be such, having no votes, and never seeing a newspaper from one year's end to the other?

It was to the Brewsters that the village was indebted for the ministry of the Rev. John Phillip, who married the sister of the pious and learned Dr. Ames, Professor of the University of Franeker. Calamy tells us that by means of Dr. Ames, Mr. Phillip had no small furtherance in his studies, and intimate acquaintance with him increased his inclination to the Congregational way. Archbishop Abbot, writing to Winwood, 1611, says: 'I have written to Sir Horace Vere touching the English preacher at the Hague. We heard what he was that preceded, and we cannot be less cognisant what Mr. Ames is, for by a Latin printed book he hath laden the Church and State of England with p. 10a great deal of infamous contumely, so that if he were amongst us he would be so far from receiving preferment, that some exemplary punishment would be his reward. His Majesty had been advertised how this man is entertained and embraced at the Hague, and how he is a fit person to breed up captains and soldiers there in mutiny and faction.' One of Dr. Ames's works, which got him into trouble, was entitled 'A Fresh Suit against Ceremonies,' a work which we may be sure would be as distasteful to the Ritualists of our day as it was to the Ritualists of his own. One of his works, his 'Medulla Theologif,' I believe, adorned the walls of the paternal study. There is, belonging to the Wrentham Congregational Church Library, a volume of tracts, sixty-seven in number, of six or eight pages each, printed in 1622, forming a series of theses on theological topics, maintained by different persons, under the presidency of Dr. Ames; and I believe a son of the Doctor is buried in Wrentham Churchyard, as I recollect my father, on one occasion, had an old gravestone done up and relettered, which bore testimony to the virtues and piety and learning of an Ames. Thus if Mr. Phillip was chased out of Old England into New England for his Nonconformity, some of the good p. 11old Noncons remained to uphold the lamp which was one day to cast a sacred light on all quarters of the land. That some did emigrate with their pastor is probable, since we learn that there is a town called Wrentham across the Atlantic, said to have received that name because some of the first settlers came from Wrentham in England.

Touching Mr. Phillip, a good deal has been written by the Rev. John Browne, the painstaking author of 'The History of Congregationalism in Suffolk and Norfolk.' It appears that his arrival in America was not unexpected, as the Christian people of Dedham had invited him to that plantation beforehand. He did not, however, accept their invitation, but being much in request, 'and called divers ways, could not resolve; but, at length, upon weighty reasons concerning the public service and foundations of the college, he was persuaded to attend to the call of Cambridge;' and, adds an American writer, 'he might have been the first head of that blessed institution.' On the calling of the Long Parliament, he and his wife returned to England, and in 1642 we find him ministering to his old flock. So satisfied were the neighbouring Independents of his Congregationalism, that when, in 1644, members of Mr. p. 12Bridge's church residing in Norwich desired to form themselves into a separate community, they not only consulted with their brethren in Yarmouth, but with Mr. Phillip also, as the only man then in their neighbourhood on whose judgment and experience they could rely. In 1643 Mr. Phillip was appointed one of the members of the Assembly of Divines, and was recognised by Baillie in his Letters as one of the Independent men there. The Independents, as we know, sat apart, and were a sad thorn in the Presbyterians' side. Five of them, more zealous than the rest, formally dissented from the decisions of the Assembly, and afraid that toleration would not be extended to them, appealed to Parliament, 'as the most sacred refuge and asylum for mistaken and misjudged innocence.' Mr. Phillip's name, however, I do not find in that list; and possibly he was too old to be very active in the matter. He lived on till 1660, when he died at the good old age of seventy-eight. In the later years of his ministry he was assisted by his nephew, W. Ames, who in 1651 preached a sermon at St. Paul's, before the Lord Mayor and Aldermen, 'On the Saint's Security against Seducing Sports, or the

Anointing from the Holy One.' It is to be feared, in our p. 13more enlightened age, a good Wrentham Congregational minister would have little chance of preaching before a London Lord Mayor. Talent is supposed to exist only in the crowded town, where men have no time to think of anything but of the art of getting on.

Other heroic associations—of men who had suffered for the faith, who feared God rather than man, who preferred the peace of an approving conscience to the vain honours of the world—also were connected with the place. I remember being shown a bush in which the conventicle preacher used to hide himself when the enemy, in the shape of the myrmidons of Bishop Wren, of Norwich, were at his heels. That furious prelate, as many of us know, drove upwards of three thousand persons to seek their bread in a foreign land. Indeed, to such an extent did he carry out his persecuting system, that the trade and manufactures of the country materially suffered in consequence. However, in my boyish days I was not troubled much about such things. Dissent in Wrentham was quite respectable. If we had lost the Brewster family, whose arms were still to be seen on the Communion plate, a neighbouring squire attended at the meeting-house, as it was p. 14then the fashion to call our chapel, and so did the leading grocer and draper of the place, and the village doctor, the father of six comely daughters; and the display of gigs on a Sunday was really imposing. Alas! as I grew older I saw that imposing array not a little shorn of its splendour. The neighbouring baronet, Sir Thomas Gooch, M.P., added as he could farm to farm, and that a Dissenter was on no account to have one of his farms was pretty well understood. I fancy our great landlords have, in many parts of East Anglia, pretty well exterminated Dissent, to the real injury of the people all around. I write this advisedly. I dare say the preaching in the meeting-house was often very miserably poor. The service, I must own, seemed to me often peculiarly long and unattractive. There was always that long prayer which was, I fear, to all boys a time of utter weariness; but, nevertheless, there was a moral and intellectual life in our Dissenting circle that did not exist elsewhere. It was true we never attended dinners at the village public-house, nor indulged in card-parties, and regarded with a horror, which I have come to think unwholesome, the frivolity of balls or the attractions of a theatre; but we had all the new books voted into our bookclub, p. 15and, as a lad, I can well remember how I revelled in the back numbers of the *Edinburgh Review*, though even then I could not but feel the injustice which it did to what it called the Lake school of poets, and more especially to Coleridge and Wordsworth. Shakespeare also was almost a sealed book, and perhaps we had a little too much of religious reading, such as Doddridge's 'Rise and Progress,' or Baxter's 'Saint's Rest,' or Alleine's 'Call to the Unconverted,' or Fleetwood's 'Life of Christ'—excellent books in their way, undoubtedly, but not remarkably attractive to boys redolent of animal life, who had thriven and grown fat in that rustic village, on whose vivid senses the world that now is produced far more effect than the terrors or splendours of the world to come.

The country round, if flat, was full of interesting associations. At the back of us—that is, on the sea—was the village of Covehithe, and when a visitor found his way into the place—an event which happened now and then—our first excursion with him or her—for plenty of donkeys were to be had which ladies could ride—was to Covehithe, known to literary men as the birthplace of John Bale, Bishop of Ossory, in Ireland. In connection with donkeys, I have this interesting recollection, p. 16that one of the old men of the village told me. At the time of the Bristol riots, he remembered Sir Charles Wetherall, the occasion of them, as a boy at Wrentham much given to donkey-riding. In the history of the drama John Bale takes distinguished rank. He was one of those by whom the drama was gradually evolved, and all to whom it is a study and delight must remember him with regard. His play of 'Kynge John' is described by Mr. Collier as occupying an intermediate place between moralities and historical plays—and it is the only known existing specimen of that species of composition of so early a date. Bale, who was trained at the monastery of White Friars, in Norwich, thence went to Jesus College, Cambridge, and was expelled in consequence of the zeal with which he exposed the errors of Popery. However, Bale had a friend and protector in Cromwell, Henry VIII.'s faithful servant. On the death of that nobleman Bale proceeded to Germany, where he appears to have been well received and hospitably entertained by Luther and Melancthon, and on the accession of Edward VI. he returned to England. In Mary's reign persecution recommenced, and Bale fled to Frankfort. He again returned at the commencement of Elizabeth's reign, and p. 17was made prebend of Canterbury, at which place he died at the age of sixty-three. Covehithe nowadays is not interesting so much as the birthplace of Bale, as on account of its ecclesiastical ruins, which are covered with ivy and venerable in their decay. The church was evidently almost a cathedral, and surely at one time or other there must have been an enormous population to worship in such a sanctuary; and yet all you see now is a public-house just opposite the church, a few cottages, and a farmhouse. A few steps farther bring you to the low cliff, and there is the sea ever encroaching on the land in that quarter and swallowing up farmhouse and farm. Miss Agnes Strickland, who lived at Reydon Hall—a few miles inland—has thus sung the melancholy fate of Covehithe:

'All roofless now the stately pile,
And rent the arches tall,
Through which with bright departing smile
The western sunbeams fall.

* * * * *

'Tradition's voice forgets to tell
Whose ashes sleep below,
And Fancy here unchecked may dwell,
And bid the story flow.'

Ah! what was that story? How the question puzzled my young head, as I walked in the sandy p. 18lane that led from my native village! How insignificant looked the little church built up inside! What had become of the crowds that at one time must have filled that ancient fane? How was it that no trace of them remained? They had vanished in the historical age, and yet no one could tell how or when. Nature was, then, stronger than man. He was gone, but the stars glittered by night and the sun shone by day, and the ivy had spread its green mantle over all. Yes! what was man, with his pomp and glory, but dust and ashes, after all! How I loved to go to Covehithe and climb its ruins, and dream of the distant past!

Here in that eastern point of England it seemed to me there was a good deal of decay. Sometimes, on a fine summer day, we would take a boat and sail from the pretty little town of Southwold, about four miles from Wrentham, to Dunwich, another relic of the past.

According to an old historian, it was a city surrounded with a stone wall having brazen gates; it had fifty-two churches, chapels, and religious houses; it also boasted hospitals, a huge palace, a bishop's seat, a mayor's mansion, and a Mint. Beyond it a forest appears to have extended some miles into what is now the sea. p. 19One of our local Suffolk poets, James Bird (I saw him but once, when I walked into his house, about twelve miles from Wrentham, having run away from home at the ripe age of ten, and told him I had come to see him, as he was a poet; and I well remember how then, much to my chagrin, he gave me plum-pudding for dinner, and sent me to play with his boys till a cart was found in which the prodigal was compelled to return), wrote and published a poetical romance, called 'Dunwich; or, a Tale of the Splendid City;' and Agnes Strickland also made it the subject of her melodious verse, commencing:

> 'Oft gazing on thy craggy brow,
> We muse on glories o'er.
> Fair Dunwich! Thou art lonely now,
> Renowned and sought no more.'

Never has a splendid city more utterly collapsed. After a long ride over sandy lanes and fields, you come to the edge of a cliff, on which stand a few houses. There is all that remains of the Dunwich where the first Bishop of East Anglia taught the Christian faith, and where was born John Daye, the printer of the works of Parker, Latimer, and Fox, who, in the reign of Mary, became, as most real men did then, a prisoner and an exile for the p. 20truth. He has also the reputation of being the first in England who printed in the Saxon character. In the records of type-founding the name of Daye stands with that of the most illustrious. When the Company of Stationers obtained their charter from Philip and Mary, he was the first person admitted to their livery. In 1580 he was master of the company, to which he bequeathed property at his death. The following is the inscription which marks the place of his burial in Little Bradley, Suffolk:

> 'Here lyes the Daye that darkness could not blynd,
> When Popish fogges had overcast the sunne;
> This Daye the cruel night did leave behind,
> To view and show what bloudie actes were donne.

He set a Fox to write how martyrs runne
By death to lyfe, Fox ventured paynes and health.
To give them light Daye spent in print his wealth,
But God with gayne returned his wealth agayne,
And gave to him as he gave to the poore.
Two wyfes he had partakers of his payne:
Each wyfe twelve babes, and each of them one
more,
Als was the last increaser of his store;
Who, mourning long for being left alone,
Sett up this tombe, herself turned to a stone.'

Unlike Covehithe, Dunwich has a history. In the reign of Henry II., a MS. in the British Museum tells us, the Earl of Leicester came to attack it. 'When he came neare and beheld the p. 21strength thereof, it was terror and feare unto him to behold it; and so retired both he and his people.' Dunwich aided King John in his wars with the barons, and thus gained the first charter. In the time of Edward I. it had sixteen fair ships, twelve barks, four-and-twenty fishing barks, and at that time there were few seaports in England that could say as much. It served the same King in his wars with France with eleven ships of war, well furnished with men and munition. In most of these ships were seventy-two men-at-arms, who served thirteen weeks at their own cost and charge. Dunwich seems to have suffered much by the French wars. Four of the eleven ships already referred to were captured by the French, and in the wars waged by Edward III. Dunwich lost still more shipping, and as many as 500 men. Perhaps it might have flourished till this day had if not been for the curse of war. But the sea also served the town cruelly. That spared nothing—not the King's Forest, where there were hawking and hunting—not the homes where England nursed her hardy sailors—not even the harbour whence the brave East Anglians sailed away to the wars. In Edward III.'s time, at one fell swoop, the remorseless sea seems to have swallowed up '400 houses p. 22which payde rente to the towne towards the fee-farms, besydes certain shops and windmills.' Yet, when I was a lad, this wreck of a place returned two members to Parliament, and Birmingham, Manchester and Sheffield not one. Between Covehithe and Dunwich stood, and still stands, the charming little bathing-place of Southwold. Like them, it has seen better days, and has suffered from the encroachments of the ever-restless and ever-hungry sea. It was at Southwold that I first saw the sea, and I remember naturally asking my father, who showed me the guns on the gun-hill — pointing seaward — whether that was where the enemies came from.

Southwold appears to have initiated an evangelical alliance, which may yet be witnessed if ever a time comes of reasonable toleration on religious matters. In many parts of the Continent the same place of worship is used by different religious bodies. In Brussels I have seen the Episcopalians, the Germans, the French Protestants, all assembling at different times in the same building. There was a time when a similar custom prevailed in Southwold, and that was when Master Sharpen, who had his abode at Sotterley, preached at Southwold once a month. There were Independents in the towns in p. 23those days, and 'his indulgence,' writes a local historian, 'favoured the Separatists with the liberty and free use of the church, where they resorted weekly, or oftener, and every fourth Sunday both ministers met and celebrated divine service alternately. He that entered the church first had the precedency of officiating, the other keeping silence until the congregation received the Benediction after sermon.' Most of the people attended all the while. It was before the year 1680 that these things were done. After that time there came to the church 'an orthodox man, who suffered many ills, and those not the lightest, for his King and for his faith, and he compelled the Independents not only to leave the church, but the town also. We read they assembled in a malt-house beyond the bridge, where, being disturbed, they chose more private places in the town until liberty of conscience was granted, when they publicly assembled in a fish-house converted to a place of worship.' At that time many people in the town were Dissenters; but it was not till 1748 that they had a church formed. Up to that time the Southwold Independents were members of the Church at Wrentham, one of the Articles of Association of the new church being to take the Bible as their sole p. 24guide, and when in difficulties to resort to the neighbouring pastor for advice and declaration. Such was Independency when it flourished all over East Anglia.

A writer in the *Harleian Miscellany* says that 'Southwold, of sea-coast town, is the most beneficial unto his Majesty of all the towns in England, by reason all their trade is unto Iceland for lings.' In the little harbour of Southwold you see nowadays only a few colliers, and I fear that the place is of little advantage to her Majesty, however beneficial it may be as a health-resort for some of her Majesty's subjects. It is a place, gentle reader, where you can wander undisturbed at your own sweet will, and can get your cheeks fanned by breezes unknown in London. The beach, I own, is shingly, and not to be compared with the sands of Yarmouth and Lowestoft; but, then, you are away from the Cockney crowds that now infest these places at the bathing season, and you are quiet—whether you wander on its common, till you come to the Wolsey Bridge, getting on towards Halesworth, where, if tradition be trustworthy, Wolsey, as a butcher's boy, was nearly drowned, and where he benevolently caused a bridge to be erected for the safety of all future butcher-boys and others, p. 25when he became a distinguished man; or ramble by the seaside to Walberswick, across the harbour, or on to Easton Bavent—another decayed village, on the other side. Southwold has its historical associations. Most of my readers have seen the well-known picture of Solebay Fight at Greenwich Hospital. Southwold overlooks the bay on which that fight was won. Here, on the morning of the 28th May, 1672, De Ruyter, with his Dutchmen, sailed right against those wooden walls which have guarded old England in many a time of danger, and found to his cost how invincible was British pluck. James, Duke of York—not then the drivelling idiot who lost his kingdom for a Mass, but James, manly and high-spirited, with a Prince's pride and a sailor's heart—won a victory that for many a day was a favourite theme with all honest Englishmen, and especially with the true and stout men who, alarmed by the roar of cannon, as the sound boomed along the blue waters of that peaceful bay, stood on the Southwold cliff, wishing that the fog which intercepted their view might clear off, and that they might welcome as victors their brethren on the sea. I can remember how, when an old cannon was dragged up from the depths of the sea, it was supposed to be, as p. 26it might have been, used in that fight, and now is preserved at one of the look-out houses on the cliff as a souvenir of that glorious struggle. The details of that fight are matters of history, and I need not dwell on them. Our literature, also, owes Southwold one of the happiest effusions of one of the wittiest writers of that age; and in a county history I remember well a merry song on the Duke's late glorious success over the Dutch, in Southwold Bay, which commences with the writer telling—

> 'One day as I was sitting still
> Upon the side of Dunwich Hill,
> And looking on the ocean,
> By chance I saw De Ruyter's fleet
> With Royal James's squadron meet;
> In sooth it was a noble treat
> To see that brave commotion.'

The writer vividly paints the scene, and ends as follows:

> 'Here's to King Charles, and here's to James,
> And here's to all the captains' names,
> And here's to all the Suffolk dames,
> And here's to the house of Stuart.'

Well, as to the house of Stuart, the less said the better; but as to the Suffolk dames, I agree with the poet, that they are all well worthy of the toast, and it was at a very early period of my existence p. 27that I became aware of that fact. But the course of true love never does run smooth, and from none—and they were many—with whom I played on the beach as a boy, or read poetry to at riper years, was it my fate to take one as wife for better or worse. In the crowded city men have little time to fall in love. Besides, they see so many fresh faces that impressions are easily erased. It is otherwise in the quiet retirement of a village where there is little to disturb the mind—perhaps too little. I can well remember a striking illustration of this in the person of an old farmer, who lived about three miles off, and at whose house we—that is, the whole family—passed what seemed to me a very happy day among the haystacks or harvest-fields once or twice a year. The old man was proud of his farm, and of everything connected with it. 'There, Master James,' he was wont to say to me after dinner, 'you can see three barns all at once!' and sure enough, looking in the direction he pointed, there were three barns plainly visible to the naked eye. Alas! the love of the picturesque had not been developed in my bucolic friend, and a good barn or two—he was an old bachelor, and, I suppose, his heart had never been softened by the love of woman—seemed to him p. 28about as beautiful an object as you could expect or desire. One emotion, that of fear, was, however, I found, strongly planted in the village breast. The boys of the village, with whom, now and then, I stole away on a birds'-nesting expedition, would have it that in a little wood about a mile or two off there were no end of flying serpents and dragons to be seen; and I can well remember the awe which fell upon the place when there came a rumour of the doings of those wretches, Burke and Hare, who were said to have made a living by murdering victims—by placing pitch plasters on their mouths—and selling them to the doctors to dissect. At this time a little boy had not come home at the proper time, and the mother came to our house lamenting. The good woman was in tears, and refused to be comforted. There had been a stranger in the village that day; he had seen her boy, he had put a pitch plaster on his mouth, and no doubt his dead body was then on its way to Norwich to be sold to the doctor. Unfortunately, it turned out that the boy was alive and well, and lived to give his poor mother a good deal of trouble. Another thing, of which I have still a vivid recollection, was the mischief wrought by Captain Swing. In Kent there had been an p. 29alarming outbreak of the peasantry, ostensibly against the use of agricultural machinery. They assembled in large bodies, and visited the farm buildings of the principal landed proprietors, demolishing the threshing machines then being brought into use. In some instances they set fire to barns and corn-stacks. These outrages spread throughout the county, and fears were entertained that they would be repeated in other agricultural districts. A great meeting of magistrates and landed gentry was held in Canterbury, the High Sheriff in the chair, when a reward was offered of #100 for the discovery of the perpetrators of the senseless mischief, and the Lords of the Treasury offered a further reward of the same amount for their apprehension; but all was in vain to stop the growing evil. The agricultural interest was in a very depressed state, and the number of unemployed labourers so large, that apprehensions were entertained that the combinations for the destruction of machinery might, if not at once checked, take dimensions it would be very difficult for the Government to control. When Parliament opened in 1830, the state of the agricultural districts had been daily growing more alarming. Rioting and incendiarism had spread from Kent to

Suffolk, p. 30Norfolk, Surrey, Hampshire, Wiltshire, Berkshire, Buckinghamshire, Huntingdonshire, and Cambridgeshire, and a great deal of very valuable property had been destroyed. A mystery enveloped these proceedings that indicated organization, and it became suspected that they had a political object. Threatening letters were sent to individuals signed 'Swing,' and beacon fires communicated from one part of the country to the other. With the object of checking these outrages, night patrols were established, dragoons were kept in readiness to put down tumultuous meetings, and magistrates and clergymen and landed gentry were all at their wits' ends. Even in our out-of-the-way corner of East Anglia not a little consternation was felt. We were on the highroad nightly traversed by the London and Yarmouth Royal Mail, and thus, more or less, we had communications with the outer world. Just outside of our village was Benacre Hall, the seat of Sir Thomas Gooch, one of the county members, and I well remember the boyish awe with which I heard that a mob had set out from Yarmouth to burn the place down. Whether the mob thought better of it, or gave up the walk of eighteen miles as one to which they were not equal, I am not in a position to say. All p. 31I know is, that Benacre Hall, such as it is, remains; but I can never forget the feeling of terror with which, on those dark and dull winter nights, I looked out of my bedroom window to watch the lurid light flaring up into the black clouds around, which told how wicked men were at their mad work, how fiendish passion had triumphed, how some honest farmer was reduced to ruin, as he saw the efforts of a life of industry consumed by the incendiary's fire. It was long before I ceased to shudder at the name of 'Swing.'

The dialect of the village was, I need not add, East Anglian. The people said 'I woll' for 'I will'; 'you warn't' for 'you were not,' and so on. A girl was called a 'mawther,' a pitcher a 'gotch,' a 'clap on the costard' was a knock on the head, a lad was a 'bor.' Names of places especially were made free with. Wangford was 'Wangfor,' Covehithe was 'Cothhigh,' Southwold was 'Soul,' Lowestoft was 'Lesteff,' Halesworth was 'Holser,' London was 'Lunun.' People who lived in the midland counties were spoken of as living in the shires. The 'o,' as in 'bowls,' it is specially difficult for an East Anglian to pronounce. A learned man was held to be a 'man of larnin',' a thing of which there was not too much in Suffolk in my p. 32young days. A lady in the village sent her son to school, and great was the maternal pride as she called in my father to hear how well her son could read Latin, the reading being reading alone, without the faintest attempt at translation. Sometimes it was hard to get an answer to a question, as when a Dissenting minister I knew was sent for to visit a sick man. 'My good man,' said he, 'what induced you to send for me?' 'Hey, what?' said the invalid. 'What induced you to send for me?' Alas! the question was repeated in vain. At length the wife interfered: 'He wants to know what the deuce you sent for him for.' And then, and not till then, came an appropriate reply. This story, I believe, has more than once found its way into *Punch*; but I heard it as a Suffolk boy years and years before *Punch* had come into existence.

One of the prayers familiar to my youth was as follows:

'Matthew, Mark, Luke, and John,
Bless the bed that I lie on;
Four corners to my bed,
Four angels at my head;
Two to watch and one to pray,
And one to carry my soul away.'

An M.P., who shall be nameless, supplies me with an apt illustration of East Anglian dialect. It p. 33was at the anniversary of a National School, with the great M.P. in the chair, surrounded by the benevolent ladies and the select clergy of the district. The subject of examination was Christ's entry into Jerusalem on an ass's colt. 'Why,' said the M.P.—'why did they strew rushes before the Saviour? can any of you children tell me?' Profound silence. The M.P. repeated the question. A little ragamuffin held up his hand. The M.P. demanded silence as the apt scholar proceeded with his answer. 'Why were the rushes strewed?' said the M.P. in a condescending tone. I don't know,' replied the boy, 'unless it was to hull the dickey down.'

Roars of laughter greeted the reply, as all the East Anglians present knew that 'hull' meant 'throw,' and 'dickey' is Suffolk for 'donkey,' but some of the Cockney visitors present were for a while quite unable to enjoy the joke.

It is to be feared the three R's were not much patronized in East Anglia, if it be true that some forty or fifty years ago, in such a respectable town as Sudbury, it was the fashion for some fifty of the leading inhabitants to meet in the large bar-parlour of the old White Horse to hear the leading paper of the eastern counties read out by a scholar and p. 34elocutionist known as John. For the discharge of this important duty he was paid a pound a year, and provided with as much free liquor as he liked, and there were people who considered that the Saturday newspaper-reading did them more good than what they heard at church the next day.

In some cases our East Anglian dialect is merely a survival of old English, as when we say 'axe' for 'ask.' We find in Chaucer:

'It is but foly and wrong wenging
To axe so outrageous thing.'

In his 'Envious Man,' Gowing made 'axeth' to rhyme with 'taxeth.' No word is more common in Suffolk than 'fare'; a pony is a 'hobby'; a thrush is a 'mavis'; a chest is a 'kist'; a shovel is a 'skuppet'; a chaffinch is a 'spink.' If a man is upset in his mind, he tells us he is 'wholly stammed,' and the Suffolk 'yow' is at least as old as Chaucer, who wrote:

'What do you ye do there, quod she,
Come, and if it lyke yow
To daucen daunceth with us now.'

An awkward lad is 'ungain.' A good deal may be written to show that our Suffolk dialect is the nearest of all provincial dialects to that of Chaucer and the Bible, and if anyone has the audacity to p. 35contradict me, why, then, in Suffolk phraseology, I can promise him — 'a good hiding.'

I am old enough to remember how placid was the county, how stay-at-home were the people, what a sensation there was created when anyone went to London, or any stranger appeared in our midst. From afar we heard of railways; then we had a railway opened from London to Brentwood; then the railways spread all over the land, and there were farmers who did think that they had something to do with the potato disease. The change was not a pleasant one: the turnpikes were deserted; the inns were void of customers; no longer did the villagers hasten to see the coach change horses, and the bugle of the guard was heard no more. For a time the Eastern Counties Railway had a somewhat dolorous career. It was thought to be something to be thankful for when the traveller by it reached his journey's end in decent time and without an accident. Now the change is marvellous. The Great Eastern Railway stands in the foremost rank of the lines terminating in London. It now runs roundly 20,000,000 of train miles in the course of a year. It carries a larger number of passengers than any other line. It carries the London working man p. 36twelve miles in and twelve miles out for twopence a day. It is the direct means of communication with all the North of Europe by its fine steamers from Harwich. It has yearly an increased number of season-ticket-holders. On a Whit Monday it gives 125,000 excursionists a happy day in the country or by the seaside. In 1891 the number of passengers carried was 81,268,661, exclusive of season-ticket-holders. It is conspicuous now for its punctuality and freedom from accidents. It is, in short, a model of good management, and it also deserves credit for looking well after the interests of its employis, of whom there are some 25,000. It contributes to the Accident Fund, to the Provident Society, to the Superannuation Fund, and to the Pension Fund, to which the men also subscribe, in the most liberal manner, and besides has established a savings bank, which returns the men who place their money in it four per cent. It is a liberal master. It does its duty to its men, who deserve well of the public as of the Great Eastern Railway itself; but its main merit, after all, is that it has been the making of East Anglia.

p. 37CHAPTER II.
the stricklands.

Reydon Hall — The clergy — Pakefield — Social life in a village.

As I write I have lying before me a little book called 'Hugh Latimer; or, The School-boy's Friendship,' by Miss Strickland, author of the 'Little Prisoner,' 'Charles Grant,' 'Prejudice and Principle,' 'The Little Quaker.' It bears the imprint — 'London: Printed for A. R. Newman and Co., Leadenhall Street.' On a blank page inside I find the following: 'James Ewing Ritchie, with his friend Susanna's affectionate regards.' Susanna was a sister of Miss Agnes Strickland, the authoress, and was as much a writer as herself. The Stricklands were a remarkable family, living about four or five miles from Wrentham, on the road leading from Wangford to Southwold, at an old-fashioned residence called Reydon Hall. They had, I fancy, seen better days, and were none the worse for that. The Stricklands came over p. 38with William the Conqueror. One of them was the first to land, and hence the name. A good deal of blue blood flowed in their veins. Kate — to my eyes the fairest of the lot — was named Katherine Parr, to denote that she was a descendant of one of the wives of the too-much-married Henry VIII., and in the old-fashioned drawing-room of Reydon Hall I heard not a little — they all talked at once — of what to me was strange and rare. Mr. Strickland had deceased some years, and the widow and the daughters kept up what little state they could; and I well remember the feeling of surprise with which I first entered their capacious drawing-room — a room the size of which it had never entered into my head to conceive of. It is to the credit of these Misses Strickland that they did not vegetate in that old house, but held a fair position in the world of letters. Miss Strickland herself chiefly resided in town. Agnes, the next, whose 'Queens of England' is still a standard book, was more frequently at home. The only one of the family who did not write was Sarah, who married one of the Radical Childses of Bungay, and who not till after the death of her husband became respectable and atoned for her sins by marrying a clergyman. p. 39Kate, as I have said, the fairest of the whole, married an officer in the army of the name of Traill, and went out to Canada, and wrote there a book called 'The

Backwoods of Canada,' which was certainly one of the most popular of the four-and-sixpenny volumes published under the auspices of the Society for the Diffusion of Useful and Entertaining Knowledge. Our friend was Susanna, who wrote a volume of poems on Enthusiasm, and who seemed to me, with her dark eyes and hair, a very enthusiastic personage indeed. The reason of her friendship with our family was her deeply religious nature, which impelled her to leave the cold and careless service of the Church—not a little to the disgust of her aristocratic sisters, who, as of ancient lineage, not a little haughty, and rank Tories, had but little sympathy with Dissent.. Susanna was much at our house, and when away scarcely a day passed on which she did not write some of us a letter or send us a book. Then there was a brother Tom, a midshipman—a wonderful being to my inexperienced eyes—who once or twice came to our house seated in the family donkey-chaise, which seemed to me, somehow or other, not to be an ordinary donkey-chaise, but something of a far superior character. I have p. 40pleasant recollections of them all, and of the annuals in which they all wrote, and a good many of which fell to my share. Like her sister, Susanna married an officer in the army—a Major Moodie—and emigrated to Canada, where the Stricklands have now a high position, where she had sons and daughters born to her, and wrote more than one novel which found acceptance in the English market. The Stricklands gave me quite a literary turn. When I was a small boy it was really an everyday occurrence for me to write a book or edit a newspaper, and with about as much success as is generally achieved by bookmakers and newspaper editors, whose merit is overlooked by an unthinking public. Let me say in the Stricklands I found an indulgent audience. On one occasion I remember reciting some verses of my own composition, commencing,

'I sing a song of ancient men,
Of warriors great and bold,
Of Hercules, a famous man,
Who lived in times of old.
He was a man of great renown,
A lion large he slew,
And to his memory games were kept,
Which now I tell to you,'

which they got me to repeat in their drawing-room, p. 41and which, though I say it that should not, evinced for a boy a fair acquaintance with 'Mangnall's Questions' and Pinnock's abridgment of Goldsmith's 'History of Rome.' Happily, at that time, Niebuhr was unknown, and sceptical criticism had not begun its deadly work. We had not to go far for truth then. It was quite unnecessary to seek it—at any rate, so it seemed to us—at the bottom of a well; there it was right underneath one's nose—before one's very eyes in the printed pages of the printed book.

Agnes Strickland did all she could to confer reputation on her native county. The tall, dark, self-possessed lady from Reydon Hall was a lion everywhere. On one occasion she visited the House of Lords, just after she had written a violent letter against Lord Campbell, charging him with plagiarism. Campbell tells us he had a conversation with her, which speedily turned her into a friend. He adds: 'I thought Brougham would have died with envy when I told him the result of my interview, and Ellenborough, who was sitting by, lifted his hands in admiration. Brougham had thrown me a note across the table, saying: "So you know your friend Miss Strickland has come to hear you."' Miss Strickland often p. 42visited Alison, the historian, at Possil House. He says of her that she had strong talents of a masculine rather than feminine character—indefatigable perseverance, and that ardour in whatever pursuit she engaged in without which no one could undergo similar fatigue. On one occasion she was descanting on the noble feeling of Queen Mary, 'That may all be very true, Miss Strickland,' replied the historian; 'but unfortunately she had an awkward habit of burning people—she brought 239 men, women, and children to the stake in a reign which did not extend beyond a few years!' 'Oh yes,' was her reply, 'it was terrible, dreadful, but it was the fault of the age—the temper of the times; Mary herself was everything that is noble and heroic.' Such was her feminine tendency to hero-worship. Another tendency of a feminine character was her love of talking. 'She did,' instances Sir Archibald, 'not even require an answer or a sign of mutual intelligence; it was enough if the one she was addressing simply remained passive. One day when I was laid up at Possil on my library sofa from a wound in the knee, she was kind enough to sit with me for two hours, and was really very entertaining, from the number of anecdotes she remembered of queens in p. 43the olden time. When she left the room she expressed herself kindly to Mrs. Alison as to the agreeable time she had spent, and the latter said to me on coming in, "What did you get to say to Miss Strickland all this time? She says you were so agreeable, and she was two hours here." "Say!" I replied with truth; "I assure you I did not say six words to her the whole time."' Agnes was a terrible one to talk—as, indeed, all the Stricklands were. In Suffolk such accomplished conversationalists were rare.

It must have been, now I come to think of it, a dismal old house, suggestive of rats and dampness and mould, that Reydon Hall, with its scantily furnished rooms and its unused attics and its empty barns and stables, with a general air of decay all over the place, inside and out. It had a dark, heavy roof and whitewashed walls, and was externally anything but a showy place, standing, as it did, a little way from the road. It must have been a difficulty with the family to keep up the place, and the style of living was altogether plain; yet there I heard a good deal of literary life in London, of Thomas Pringle, the poet, and the Secretary of the Anti-Slavery Society, whose 'Residence in South Africa' is still one of the p. 44most interesting books on that quarter of the world, and of whom Josiah Conder, one of the great men of my smaller literary world at that time, wrote an appreciative biographical sketch. Mr. Pringle, let me remind my readers, was the original editor of *Blackwood's Magazine*, a magazine which still maintains its reputation as being the best of its class. Mr. Pringle, I believe, at some time or other, had visited Wrentham; at any rate, the Stricklands, especially Susanna, were among his intimate friends, and, from what I heard, I could well believe, when, at a later period, I visited his grave in Bunhill Fields, what I found recorded there—that 'In the walks of British literature he was known as a man of genius; in the domestic circle he was loved as an affectionate relative and faithful friend; in the wide sphere of humanity he was revered as the advocate and protector of the oppressed,' who 'left among the children of the African desert a memorial of his philanthropy, and bequeathed to his fellow-countrymen an example of enduring virtue.' At the home of the Pringles the Stricklands made many literary acquaintances, such as Alaric Watts, and Mrs. S. C. Hall, and others of whom I heard them talk. At that time, however, literature was not, as far as women were p. 45concerned, the lucrative profession it has since become, and I have a dim remembrance of their paintings—for in this respect the Stricklands, like my own mother, were very accomplished—being sold at the Soho Bazaar, a practice which helped to maintain them in the respectability and comfort becoming their position in life. But in London they never forgot the old home, and wrote so much about it in their stories, that there was not a flower, or shrub, or tree, or hedge, or mossy bank redolent in early spring of primroses and violets, to which they had not given, to my boyish eyes, a glory and a charm. This reference to painting reminds me of a feature of my young days, not without interest, in connection with the name of Cunningham—a name at one time well known in the religious world.

The reader must be reminded that the reverend gentleman referred to was a *rara avis*, and that between him and the neighbouring clergy there was little sympathy—unless the common rallying cry of 'The Church in Danger!' was raised as an electioneering dodge. The clergyman at Wrentham at that time, who declared himself the appointed vessel of grace for the parish, I have been led to believe, since I have become older, was by no p. 46means a saint, and his brethren were notorious as evil-livers. Some twenty years ago one of them had his effects sold off, and his library was viewed with no little amusement by his parishioners, to many of whom, if popular fame be an authority, he was more than a spiritual father. The library contained only one book that could be called theological, and the title of that wonderfully unique volume was, 'Die and be Damned; or, An End of the Methodists.' All the other books were exclusively sporting, while the pictures were such as would have been a disgrace to Holywell Street. It was of him that the clerk said that 'next Sunday there would be no Divine sarvice, as maaster was going to Newmarket.' Once upon a time after a sermon one of his flock approached him, as he had been preaching on miracles, to ask him to explain what a miracle really was. The reverend gentleman gave his rustic inquirer a kick, adding, 'Did you feel that?'

'Oh yes, sir; but what of that?'

'Why,' said the reverend gentleman, 'if you had not felt it, it would have been a miracle, that is all.' Yet that man was as popular as any parson in the district, perhaps more so, and it was with some indignation in certain quarters that the people p. 47learned that a new Bishop had come to Norwich, and that the parson had been deprived of his living for immoral conduct. Of another it is said that, calling on a poor villager, dying and full of gloomy anticipations as to the future, all he could say was, 'Don't be frightened; I dare say you will meet a good many people you know.' I have often heard old men talk of the time when they used to take the parson home in a wheelbarrow — but that was before we had a Sunday-school, at which I was a regular teacher. The church had a Sunday-school, but not till after the one in the chapel had existed many years. Of these ornaments of the Church and foes of Dissent, some had apparently a sense of shame — one of them, at any rate, committed suicide.

At Pakefield, some seven miles from Wrentham, and just on the borders of Lowestoft, then, as now, the most eastern extremity of England, resided the Rev. Francis Cunningham. He was a clergyman of piety and philanthropy, rare at that time in that benighted district, and in this respect he was aided by his wife, a little dark woman whom I well remember, a sister of the far-famed John Joseph Gurney, of Earlham. It is with pleasure I quote the following from the Journal of Caroline p. 48Fox: 'A charming story of F. Cunningham coming in to prayers just murmuring something about the study being on fire, and proceeding to read a long chapter and make equally long comments thereupon. When the reading was over, and the fact became public, he observed, "Yes, I saw it was a little on fire, but I opened the window on leaving the room."' Mr. Cunningham had much to do with establishing a branch of the British and Foreign Bible Society in Paris in connection with the Buxtons. In this way, but on a smaller scale, the Cunninghams were equally distinguished, and one of the things they had established at Pakefield was an infant school, to which I, in company with my parents — indeed, I may add, the whole family — was taken, in order, if possible, that our little village should possess a similar institution. But my principal pilgrimages to the Pakefield vicarage were in connection with some mission to aid Oberlin in his grand work amongst the mountains and valleys of Switzerland. It appeared Mr. and Mrs. Cunningham had visited the good man, and watched him in his career, and had come back to England to gain for him, if possible, sympathy and friends. Mrs. Cunningham had taken drawings of the principal objects of p. 49interest, which had been lithographed, and these lithographs my mother, who in her way was as great an enthusiast as Susanna Strickland herself, was very anxious to obtain; the financial position of the family, however, forbade any thought of purchase. But she had a wonderful gift of painting, and she painted while we children were learning the Latin grammar, or preparing our lessons in the Delectus, much to my terror, as I had a habit of restlessness which, by shaking the table, not only impaired her work, but drew down upon me not a little of reproach; and with these paintings I was despatched on foot to Pakefield, where, in return for them, I was given the famous lithographs, which were to be preserved for many a year in the spare room we called the parlour—drawing-rooms at that time in East Anglia were, I think, unknown. What a joy it was to us children when that parlour had its fire lit, and we found out that company was coming—partly, I must add, for sensual reasons. We knew that the best tea-things were to be used, that unusual delicacies were to be placed upon the table, and I must do my mother the justice to say that she could cook as well as she could paint; but for other and higher motives, and not as an occasion p. 50of feasting or for the disuse of the economical pinafore which was always worn to keep our clothes clean, did we rejoice when we found there was to be tea in the parlour. If young people were coming, we were sure to dissect puzzles, or play some game which combined amusement with instruction; and if the party consisted of seniors, as on the occasion of the Book Club—almost all Dissenting congregations had their Book Clubs then—it was a pleasure to listen to my father's talk, who was a well-read man, and who, being a Scotchman, had inherited his full share of Scotch wit, which, however, was enlivened with quotations from 'Hudibras,' the only poet, alas! in whom he seemed to take any particular interest. There, in the parlour, were the fraternal meetings attended by all the neighbouring Independent ministers, all clad in sober black, and whose wildest exploits in rollicking debauchery were confined to a pipe and a glass of home-made wine. Madeira, port and sherry were unknown in ministers' houses, though now and then one got a taste of them at the houses of men better to do, and who, perhaps, had been as far as London once or twice in their lives. Of these neighbouring ministers, one of the most celebrated at that time was the Rev. Edward p. 51Walford, then of Yarmouth, who afterwards became tutor of Homerton College, and who, after the death of a favourite and accomplished daughter—I can still remember the gracefulness of her person—sank into a state of profound melancholy, which led him to shut himself from his friends, to give up all public preaching and tutorial work, and to consider himself as hopelessly lost. It is a curious fact that he dated his return to reason and happiness and usefulness after a visit paid him by my father, who happened to be in town, and who naturally was drawn to see his afflicted friend, with whom, in the days of auld lang syne, he had smoked many a pipe and held many an argument respecting Edwards on Freedom of the Will, and his favourite McKnight. Mrs. Walford, who was aware of my father's intended visit, had thoughtfully prepared pipes and tobacco, and placed them on the table of the room where the interview was to take place. My father went and smoked his pipe and talked as usual, poor Mr. Walford sitting sad and dejected, and refusing to be comforted all the while. When my father had left—owing, I suppose, to the force of old associations—actually the poor man approached the table, took up a pipe, filled it with tobacco, and smoked p. 52it. From that hour, strange to say, he recovered, wrote a translation of the Psalms, became a trustee of Coward's College, and took charge of a church at Uxbridge. This is 'a fac,' as Artemus Ward would say, and 'facs' are stubborn things. Of this Mr. Walford, the well-known publisher of that name in St. Paul's Churchyard was a son, and the firm of Hodder and Stoughton may be said to carry on his business, though on a larger scale.

Dressed in rusty black, with hats considerably the worse for wear, with shoes not ignorant of the cobbler's art, unconscious of and careless for the fashions of the world, rarely in London, except on the occasion of the May Meetings—no one can tell, except those who, like myself, were admitted behind the scenes, as it were, how these good men lived to keep alive the traditions of freedom, civil and religious, in districts most under the sway of the ignorant squire and the equally ignorant parson of the parish. If there has been a decency and charm about our country life it is due to them, and them alone. Perhaps, more in the country than in the crowded city is the pernicious influence felt of sons of Belial, flushed with insolence and wine. It is difficult to give the reader an idea of the utter animalism, if I may so term it, of p. 53rural life some fifty years ago. For small wages these Dissenting ministers did a noble work, in the way of preserving morals, extending education, promoting religion, and elevating the aim and tone of | the little community in which they lived, and moved, and had their being. At home the difficulties of such of them as had large families were immense. The pocket was light, and too often there was but little in the larder. But they laboured on through good and bad report, and now they have their reward. Perhaps one of their failings was that they kept too much the latter end in view, and were too indifferent to present needs and requirements. They did not try to make the best of both worlds. I can never forget a remark addressed to me by all the good men of the class with whom I was familiar in my childhood as to the need of getting on in life and earning an honest penny, and be-coming independent in a pecuniary point of view. I was to be a good boy, to love the Lord, to study the Assembly's Catechism, to read the Bible, as if outside the village there was no struggle into which sooner or later I should have to plunge—no hard battle with the world to fight, no temporal victory to win.

p. 54CHAPTER III
lowestoft.

Yarmouth bloaters — George Borrow — The town fifty years ago — The distinguished natives.

'I'm a-thinking you'll be wanting half a pint of beer by this time, won't you?'

Such were the first words I heard as I left the hotel where I was a temporary sojourner about nine o'clock. Of course I turned to look at the speaker. He wore an oilskin cap, with a great flap hanging over the back of the neck; his oilskin middle was encased in a thick blue guernsey; his trousers were hidden in heavy jack-boots, which came up above his knees; his face was red, and his body was almost as round as that of a porpoise. When I add that the party addressed was similarly adorned and was of a similar build, the reader will guess at once that I was amongst a seafaring community, and let me add that this supposition is correct. I was, in fact, at Lowestoft, and Lowestoft just now p. 55is, with Yarmouth, the headquarters of the herring fishery. The truth is, as the poet tells us, 'Things are not what they seem,' and that many of the Yarmouth bloaters which we are in the habit of indulging in at breakfast in reality come from Lowestoft.

It is worth going from London at the season of the year when the finest bloaters are being caught, to realize the peril and the enterprise and the industry connected with the herring trade, which employs some five hundred boats, manned by seven to twelve men, who work the business on the cooperative system, which, when the season is a good one, gives a handsome remuneration to all concerned, and which drains the country of young men for miles around. Each boat is furnished with some score of nets, and each net extends more than thirty-two yards. The boat puts off according to the tide, and if it gets a good haul, at once returns to the harbour with its freight; if the catch is indifferent, the boat stays out; the fish are salted as they are caught, and then the boat, generally at a distance of about twenty miles from the shore, waits till a sufficient number have been caught to complete the cargo. When that is the case, the boat at once makes for Lowestoft, and the fish are unloaded p. 56under a shed in heaps of about half a last (a last is professedly 10,000 herrings, but really much more). At nine a bell rings and the various auctioneers commence operations. A crowd is formed, and in a very few minutes a lot is sold off to traders who are well known, and who pay at the end of the week. The auctioneer then proceeds to the next group, which is disposed of in a similar way. Other auctioneers in various parts of the enormous shed erected for their accommodation do the same, and then, as more boats arrive, other cargoes are sold, the sailors bringing a hundred as a sample from the boat. And thus all day long the work of selling goes on, and as soon as a lot are sold they are packed up with ice, if fresh, or with more salt, if already salted, and despatched by train to various quarters of England, where, it is to be presumed, they meet with a speedy and immediate sale. In this way as many as one hundred and ninety-eight trucks are sometimes sent off in a single day. But in London we are familiar with the kipper, the red herring, and the Yarmouth bloater, and to see how they are prepared for consumption I leave the market—always wet and fishy and slippery—and make my way to the extensive premises on the p. 57beach belonging to Mr. Thomas Brown—the only Brown whose name is familiar to the fish-dealer in every market in England, and the extent of whose business may be best realized by the reader when I state that Mr. Brown sends off from his factory as many as forty lasts a week.

An intelligent foreman, after I have evaded the attack of a formidable dog which keeps watch and ward over the premises, explains to me the mystery of the trade. I find myself in the midst of a square. On one side are a great stack of oak and many casks of old salt. The latter, I gather, is sold to be used as manure. The former is applied to the fire, which gently smokes the Yarmouth bloater. On one side, the herrings, as they are received, are pickled—that is, first washed in fresh water, and then immersed in great tubs in which the water is mixed with salt. The next thing is to take them into a room in which several women are engaged in spitting them—that is, hanging them on rods—and then they are carried to the apartment where they are hung up, while oak logs are burnt beneath. In twelve hours they are sufficiently smoked, and then you have the real Yarmouth bloater. I am glad I have seen the process, as I have a horrible suspicion that the p. 58costermonger manufactures many a Yarmouth bloater in some filthy Whitechapel slum, the odour of which by no means tends to improve the flavour of so delicate a fish.

But we have to discuss the red-herring, not of the artful politician, anxious to dodge his hearers, but of the breakfast-table. For this purpose I am taken to a large oven filled with oak sawdust, gathered from Ipswich, and oak shavings, which are also brought from a distance, principally from Bass's Brewery, and, indeed, from all the great works where oak is used; I see heaps of fire made from these ashes, which give out much heat, and at the same time much smoke. In a loft above are hung the herrings, and there they hang twelve days, till they gradually become of the colour of a guinea, when they are packed up and sent away in casks, while the bloaters go away in baskets of a hundred, in pots holding a smaller number, and in barrels in which as many as three hundred are stowed away. As to the kippered herring, he undergoes quite a different treatment. Some twenty or thirty women get hold of him, cut him open, take out his gut and wash him, and then he is hung over an oak fire and smoked for twelve hours, and thus, saturated with smoke inside and out, is regarded in p. 59many circles as a delicacy to be highly prized. But he must be got off the premises. Well, if we climb to a loft, we shall see a good many young women hard at work stripping the rods, on which he and his fellows have been suspended, and stowing the fish away. In the autumn especially the peculiar industries connected with the trade are very considerably exercised. All day long carts come in with the fish; all day long carts go out with the manufactured articles to the railway-station; day and night the men and women are at work; in one quarter the women make and mend the nets, which are then boiled in cutch and put on board the boats; in another quarter coopers are at work making boxes and casks and barrels. As to the baskets, the country is ransacked for them, and as soon as they are filled they take the train and away they go, to give a flavour to the potato dinner of the poor man, or to form a tasty adjunct to the dishes under which the breakfast table of his lord and master groans. In London we get the best — the smaller herrings go to the North, as the dwellers in those parts will not pay the price the Londoner does. Great is the joy and rejoicing, as well can be imagined, at Lowestoft when the herring season comes on. It is true, the Lowestoft p. 60fishers do not have it all to themselves. Yarmouth is a fierce rival in the race, and, as it has now superior accommodation, many a boat makes for that far-famed port. Then, the Scotch, when they have done their fishing, make for the English coast, and manage, as Scotchmen ever do, to gather a fair share of the spoil. As to the foreigners, they are not such formidable rivals as sometimes we are apt to believe. The Frenchman or the Dutchman comes, but that is when he is blown off by a gale from his own happy hunting-ground, and then we know, all the world over, the cry is, 'Any port in a storm.'

Oh, these storms! how terrible they are! and how little, as we eat our Yarmouth bloater of a morning, or spread the bloater-paste as a covering to the thin slice of bread-and-butter, to tempt the languid appetite—how little do we who sit at home at ease realize their fury and their power! As I now write, twenty-one orphans are bewailing the loss of fathers who went out in a craft during the last gale, and of whom no sign has been seen, nor ever will. Hour by hour the women, weeping and watching on the sandy shore, saw one and another familiar boat come, more or less buffeted, into port. On more than one a hand had been washed away, p. 61but the craft and the rest of the crew were saved somehow. But one boat yet remained missing, and in vain the survivors were questioned as to what had become of the *Skimmer of the Sea*. Day by day anxious eyes swept the distant horizon. Day by day a sadder weight came down on weeping child and broken-hearted wife; and now all hope is gone, and all felt that in the fury of the gale the *Skimmer of the Sea* foundered with all her hands. Well, as the good old Admiral said, as he and his men were about to perish, 'My lads, the way to heaven is as short by sea as by land.' But the wounded heart in the agony of its grief is slow to realize that fact. Sailors ought to be serious men; every halfpenny they earn is won at the risk of a life. In Lowestoft, I am glad to find, many of them are. 'The Salvation Army has done 'em a deal of good,' says a decent woman, with whom I happened to scrape an acquaintance at the most attractive coffee-house I have ever seen—the Coffee Pot at Mutford Bridge. 'Not that I holds with the Salvation Army myself, sir, but they've done the men a deal of good, and they don't spend their wages, as they used to do, in drink.'

Lowestoft, when I was there last, had just lost p. 62one of its heroes—I mean the late Mr. George Borrow—whose 'Bible in Spain' was the talk of the season in religious and worldly circles alike, and whose writings on Gipsies and Wild Wales and the 'Bible in Spain' achieved at one time an enormous popularity. He lived—I can still remember his tall form—on a bank a couple of miles out of Lowestoft, sloping down to a large piece of water known in those parts as Oulton Broad. The tourist, if he looks to his right just after he has passed Mutford Bridge on the rail from Lowestoft to Beccles, across the wide sheet of water, which, as I saw it last, lay calm and blue in the fading glory of an autumnal sun, will perhaps see a white house at a distance, nestled in among the fir-trees—that was where George Borrow lived, and where he died, though he was buried in Brompton Cemetery by the side of his wife. You cannot make a mistake, for houses are rare in those parts. As his step-daughter observed to me, the proper way is by water; to get to the house by land—at least as I did—you walk along the rail for a couple of miles, then break off across a bit of a swamp, to a little lane that conducts you to Oulton Church—a very ancient one, which, however, is in a state of good repair and is noted partly on account of the p. 63fact that the steeple is built in the middle, and partly on account of its containing, so it is said, the earliest example of a brass to an ecclesiastic which is to be found in England. A narrow path from the church leads you to Oulton Hall, which came into the possession of Borrow by marriage, really a very plain, red-brick, capacious, comfortable-looking old farmhouse, only of a superior class. Keeping the Hall to the right, you reach a gate, which opens into a very narrow lane, full of mud in the winter and dust in the summer. The lane loses itself in the marshland, on the borders of Lake Lothing—a name supposed to have been derived from a certain Danish prince, murdered on the spot by a jealous Court retainer; and it is a fitting place for a murder, as in that lonely district there was no eye to pity, no ear to hear, no hand to save. Even to-day, as you look away from the train, there is little sign of life, save the sail of a distant wherry as it makes sluggishly for Norwich or Beccles, as it goes either into the Waveney or the Yare; or the gray wing of the heron as it flies heavily along the marsh; and that is all. Far away, perhaps, rises a ridge, with a house on it; or a steeple, with a few trees struggling to yield the barren spot a shelter from the suns of summer p. 64or the howling winds of winter; but all is still life there, and the habitations of men are few and far between. In the particular lane to which I have introduced the reader — there are but two — there is a little cottage on your left, and beyond, under a group of trees, mostly fir, which almost hide it from view, a home of a rather superior character, in a very dilapidated condition, with everything around it more or less untidy — that was where George Borrow lived and worked in his way for many a long day. The step-daughter and her husband reside there now — very ancient people, who are to be seen driving about Lowestoft in a little wicker car, drawn by an amiable and active donkey, an aged dog guarding the cottage during their temporary absence. The female, an ancient one, who did for the house, lives in the little cottage which the tourist will have already observed, and the interior of which presented, when I peeped in, a far greater idea of comfort than did Oulton Cottage, the residence of the late George Borrow. The picture one gets is rather a melancholy one. 'He was a funny-tempered man' — that seems to have been the idea of the few people around. Latterly he kept no company, and no one came to see him. All who did call on him, however, tell p. 65me that he was well dressed, but that all the interior of the house was dirty. Well, that was to be expected of a man who loved to live with the gipsies, and patter to them in Romany of Egyptian lore, for it could not have been want of means. Borrow must have made a good deal of money by his books, and I have heard his landed property estimated at five hundred per year. The house looked like the residence of a miser who would not lay out a penny in keeping up appearances or in repairs. It must be remembered, however, that the grand old man had long become bowed with age; that for some years before his death he was scarcely able to move himself without help; that the grasshopper, as it were, had become a burden. In summer time such a residence, in good repair and well furnished, would be perfectly charming. The house contains a sitting-room on each side of the entrance-hall. Behind is the kitchen, and above are four bedrooms and two attics — none of them large, I own, but at any rate capable of being made very cosy. On your right, in a little niche in the cliff, is a small stable. Lower down is a large summer-house, then full of books (amongst them, I believe, there were a hundred lexicons), where their learned proprietor loved to write. p. 66Farther down the lawn you come to the lake, where Borrow could enjoy his morning bath without fear of being disturbed, and where any amount of fish can be got. Just previous to my last visit to the spot a pike of more than twenty pounds' weight—I am afraid to say how many pounds more, lest the reader should think I was exaggerating—had been caught. For a real angler or sportsman such a house as that in which George Borrow spent the latter years of his long life must have been a perfect paradise. The world is utterly away from you, and, what is better still, in such a spot the world has no chance of finding you out. Approaching by road, you see no sign of the house till you are in it, so completely is it hidden in the nook of trees in which it stands. Only to the water is it open. It would be really beautiful to live there in the summer, and have a gondola to row into Beccles or Lowestoft or Bungay when you wanted to be gay.

One good anecdote I heard of George Borrow the last time I was in the neighbourhood, which is worth repeating. My informant was an Independent minister, at that time supplying the pulpit at Lowestoft, and staying at Oulton Hall, then inhabited by a worthy Dissenting tenant. One p. 67night a meeting of the Bible Society was held at Mutford Bridge, at which the party from the Hall attended, and where George Borrow was one of the speakers. After the meeting was over, all the speakers went back to supper at Oulton Hall, and my friend among them, who, in the course of the supper, found himself attacked very violently by the clergyman for holding Calvinistic opinions. Naturally my friend replied that the clergyman was bound to do the same. 'How do you make that out?' 'Why, the Articles of your Church are Calvinistic, and to them you have sworn assent.' 'Oh yes, but there is a way of explaining them away.' 'How so?' said my friend. 'Oh,' replied the clergyman, 'we are not bound to take the words in their natural sense.' My friend, an honest, blunt East Anglian, intimated that he did not understand that way of evading the difficulty; but he was then a young man, and did not like to continue the discussion further. However, George Borrow, who had not said a word hitherto, entered into the discussion, opening fire on the clergyman in a very unexpected manner, and giving him such a setting down as the hearers, at any rate, never forgot. All the sophistry about the non-natural meaning of terms was held up by p. 68Borrow to ridicule, even contempt; and the clergyman was beaten at every point. 'Never,' says my friend, 'did I hear one man give another such a dressing as on that occasion.' It was not always, however, that Borrow thus shone. In the neighbourhood of Bungay lived a gentleman much given to collect around him men of literary taste and culture. A lecture was to be given in the neighbourhood, and all the men of light and leading around were invited. George Borrow was one of the earliest arrivals, and seated himself before the fire with a book in his hand, over which he nodded superciliously, as the host brought up all his guests in succession to be introduced to the lion of the town. At dinner which followed, which was rather a jovial one, and at which the bottle went round freely, so loud and general was the conversation that my friend, a clever lawyer, with remarkably good ears, was quite unable to catch a sentence from the great author's lips. Perhaps Borrow really did say nothing, or next to nothing. It is quite as likely that he did as not, as I have already informed the reader that 'he was a funny-tempered man.'

'Catherine Gurney,' writes Caroline Fox, 'gave us a note to George Borrow, so on him we called— p. 69a tall, ungainly man, with great physical strength, quick, penetrating eye, a confident manner, and a disagreeable tone and pronunciation.' We gather from the same lady that it was Joseph John Gurney who recommended George Borrow to the Committee of the Bible Society. 'So he stalked up to London, and they gave him a hymn to translate into the Manchow language, and the same to one of their people to translate also. When compared they proved to be very different. When put before their reader, he had the candour to say that Borrow's was much the better of the two. On this they sent him to Petersburg to get it printed, and then gave him business in Portugal.'

One thing is clear—that Borrow was a lonely man, and evidently one who did not hold the resources of civilization in such esteem as Mr. Gladstone does. He loved Nature and her ways, and people like the gipsies, who are supposed to be of a similar way of thinking. He eschewed the hum of cities and the roar of the 'madding crowd.' He was big in body and in mind, and wanted elbow-room; and yet what would he have been if he had not lived in a city, and come under the stimulative influence of such men as Edward Taylor, of p. 70Norwich? It is idle to complain of cities, however they sully the air, and deface the land, and pollute the water, and rear the weak and vicious and the wicked — to remind us how low and depraved human nature can become when it is cut off from communion with Nature and Nature's God. Borrow owed much to cities, and was best appreciated by the men who dwelt in them. There is often a good deal of affectation about the love of rural solitude, nor does it often last long when there is a wife to have a voice in the matter. Yet in Borrow undoubtedly the feeling was sincere, and of him Wordsworth might have written —

> 'As in the eye of Nature he has lived,
> So in the eye of Nature let him die.'

Lowestoft was a frequent attraction for a youthful ramble — perhaps almost too far, unless one could manage to get a lift in a little yellow-painted black-bodied vehicle called a whisky, which was grandfather's property, and into the shafts of which could be put any spare quadruped, whether donkey, or mule, or pony, it mattered little, and which afforded a considerable relief when a trip as far as Lowestoft was determined on. At that time there was no harbour, and the town consisted simply of one High Street, gradually rising towards the north, p. 71with a fine space for boys to play in between the cliff and the sea, called the denes. I can well remember being taken to view the works of the harbour before the water was let in, and not a little astonished at what then was to me a new world of engineering science and skill. In the High Street there was a little old-fashioned and by no means flourishing Independent Chapel, where at one time the preacher was the Rev. Mr. Maurice, the father of the Mr. Maurice to whom many owe a great awakening of spiritual life, and whose memory they still regard as that of a beloved and honoured teacher. Mr. Maurice was a Unitarian, I believe, and, when he retired, handed over the chapel to my father with the remark that it was no use his preaching there any longer. The preacher in my time was the Rev. George Steffe Crisp, a kindly, timid, tearful man, always in difficulties with his people, and who often resorted to Wrentham for advice. Latterly he retired from the ministry, and kept a shop and school. In this capacity one day my old friend John Childs, of Bungay, the far-famed printer — of whom

I shall have much to say anon—called on him, when the following dialogue took place: 'Good-morning, Mr. Crisp.' 'Good-morning, Mr. Childs.' 'Well, how p. 72are you getting on?' 'Oh, very well; but there is one thing that troubles me much.' 'What is that?' 'That I am getting deaf, and can't hear my minister.' 'Oh,' was the cynical reply, 'you ought to be thankful for your privileges.'

Lowestoft is reported to have been a fishing station as early as the time of the Romans; but the ancient town is supposed to have been long engulfed by the resistless sea, for there was to be seen till the 25th of Henry VIII. the remains of an old house upon an inundated spot—left dry at low water about four furlongs east of the present beach. The town has been the birthplace of many distinguished men—of Sir Thomas Allen, for instance, who was steadily attached to the Royal cause, and who after the Restoration rose high in command, and won many a victory over the Dutch and the Algerines; of Sir Andrew Leake, who fell in the attack on Gibraltar; of Rear-Admiral Richard Utbar, also a renowned fighter when England and Holland were at war. To the same town also belong Admiral Sir John Ashby, who died in 1693, and his nephew Vice-Admiral James Mighells. Nor must we fail to do justice to Thomas Nash, a facetious writer of considerable reputation in the latter part of the sixteenth p. 73century. The most witty of his productions is a satirical pamphlet in praise of red herrings, intended as a joke upon the great staple of Yarmouth, and the pretensions of that place to superiority over Lowestoft. It must be confessed that Nash is chiefly famous as a caustic pamphleteer and an unscrupulous satirist. For illustration we may point to his battle with Gabriel Harvey, the friend of Edmund Spenser, who desired that he might be epitaphed the inventor of the not yet naturalized English hexameter; and his other battle with Martin Mar Prelate, or the writer or writers who passed under that name, and who have acquired a reputation to which poor Nash can lay no claim. His one conspicuous dramatic effort is 'Summer's Last Will and Testament.' Nash wrote for bare existence—to use his own words, 'contending with the cold, and conversing with scarcity.' Nash lived in an unpropitious age. A recent French writer has placed him in the foremost rank of English writers. Dr. Jusserand, the author referred to, in his accounts of the English novel in the time of Shakespeare, tells us Nash was the most successful exponent in England of the picturesque novel. The picturesque novel is the forerunner of the realistic novel of modern p. 74times. It portrays the life and fortunes of the picaro—the adventurer who tries all roads to fortune. Spanish in its origin, it developed into a school in which Defoe and Thackeray distinguished themselves. 'Nash,' writes the French author, 'mingled serious scenes with his comedy, in order that his romances might more nearly resemble real life.' In fact (he writes), 'Nash does not only possess the merit of learning how to observe the ridiculous side of human nature, and of portraying in a full light picturesque figures—now worthy of Teniers and now of Callot—some fat and greasy, others lean and lank; he possesses a thing very rare with the picturesque school, the faculty of being moved. He seems to have foreseen the immense field of study which was to be opened later to the novelist. A distant ancestor of Fielding, as Lilly and Sidney appear to us to be distant ancestors of Richardson, he understands that a picture of active life, reproducing only in the Spanish fashion scenes of comedy, is incomplete and departs from reality. The greatest jesters, the most arrogant, the most venturesome, have their days of anguish. No hero has ever yet remained imprisoned from the cradle to the grave, and no one has been able to live an irresponsible spectator, p. 75and not feel his heart sometimes beat the quicker, nor bow his head unmoved. Nash caught a glimpse of this.' As an illustration, Dr. Jusserand points to his 'Jack Wilton'—'The best specimen of the picturesque tale in English literature anterior to Defoe.' In Lowestoft they ought to keep his memory green.

The writer well remembers the day when Mr., afterwards Sir, Morton Peto, assembled the inhabitants of Lowestoft in the then dilapidated Town Hall, and promised that if they would sell their ruined harbour works, and back him in making a railway, their mackerel and herrings should be delivered almost alive in Manchester, Liverpool, and London. The inhabitants believed in the power of the enchanter, and Lowestoft is metamorphosed. The old town remains upon its beautiful eminence, and memory clings to the cliffs and to the denes, tenanted only, the one by wild rabbits, the other by the merry children and the nets of the fishermen. But a new town has grown up around the harbour—a grand hotel, excellent lodging-houses, a new church; a great population have upset the romance, and borne witness to the spirit of enterprise which characterizes this generation. The new town has spread to Kirkley, has Londonized even p. 76quiet Pakefield, and awakened a sleeping neighbourhood to what men call life.

At Lowestoft commence what are known to sailors as the Yarmouth Roads—a grand stretch of sea protected by the sands, where an armada might anchor secure; and it was a sight not to be seen now, when gigantic steamers do all the business of the sea, to watch the hundreds of ships that would come inside the Roads at certain seasons of the year. There, in the winter-time—that is, from Lowestoft to Covehithe—I have seen the beach strewed with wrecks, chiefly of rotten colliers, or ships in the corn trade; but inside 'Lowestoft Roads,' to which they were guided by a lighthouse on the cliff, they were supposed to be secure. Lowestoft at that time, with its charming sands, was little known to the gay world, and depended far more on the fishing than the bathing season. The former was a busy time, and kept all the country round in a state of excitement. Many were the men, for instance, who, even as far off as Wrentham, went herring or mackerel fishing in the big craft, which, drawn up on the beach when the season was over, seemed to me ships such as never had been seen by the mariners of Tyre and Sidon; but the chief interest to me were the vans p. 77in which the fish were carried from Lowestoft to London—light spring-carts with four wheels and two horses, that, after changing horses at our Spread Eagle, raced like lightning along the turnpike-road, at all hours, and even on Sundays—a sad grievance to the godly—beating the Yarmouth mail.

Now and then, even at that remote period, when railways were not, and when Lowestoft was no port, nothing but a fishing-station, distinguished people came to Lowestoft, attracted by its bracing air and exceptional bathing attractions. I can in this way recollect Sir Edward Parry and M. Guizot. But there were other personages equally distinguished. One of these was Mrs. Siddons, with whom an old Dissenting minister—the Rev. S. Sloper, of Beccles, whom I can well remember—contracted quite an intimacy. She had already passed the zenith of her celebrity. 'Providence,' writes my friend, Mr. Wilton Rix, of Beccles, in his 'East Anglian Nonconformity,' published as far back as 1851, 'had repeatedly and recently called her to tread in domestic life the path of sorrow, and her religious advantages, however few, had taught her that

'"That path alone
Leads to the land where sorrow is unknown."

p. 78'"Sweet, sometimes," said she, "are the uses of adversity. It not only strengthens family affection, but it teaches us all to walk humbly with God." It is not surprising that she was disposed to cultivate the society of those who could blend piety with cheerfulness, and with whom she might be on friendly terms without ceremony. Such acquaintances she found in Mr. Sloper's family. Mrs. Siddons, with unassuming kindness, contributed to their amusement by specimens of her powerful reading. She joined willingly in the worship of the family, and maintained the same invaluable practice at her own lodgings.' Mr. Rix continues: 'Just at that time Mr. Sloper was requested to preach to his own people on an affecting and mournful occasion, the death of a suicide. Though he keenly felt the delicacy and difficulty of the task, a sense of duty and a possibility of usefulness overcame his scruples. He selected for his text the impressive sentiment of the Apostle, "The sorrow of the world worketh death." Mrs. Siddons was one of his auditors. She, who had been the honoured guest of Royalty, who had been enthroned as the Tragic Muse, and whose voice had charmed applauding multitudes, was seen in the humble Dissenting meeting-house at Beccles shedding abundant and unaffected tears at p. 79the plain and faithful exhibition of religious truth. Mr. Sloper's preaching was as powerfully recommended to her by the delightful illustration of Christian principles exhibited in his private character, as by the intrinsic importance of those principles, and the simple gravity and penetrating earnestness with which they were announced from his lips. He afterwards procured for her, at her request, a copy of Scott's admirable "Commentary on the Bible," which he accompanied with a letter, warmly urging upon her attention the great realities her profession had so manifest a tendency to exclude from her contemplations. Mrs. Siddons,' again I quote Mr. Rix, 'more than once expressed her gratitude for the interest Mr. Sloper had evinced in her eternal welfare; she thanked him in writing for the advice he had given her, adding an emphatic wish that God might enable her to follow it—a wish which her pious and amiable correspondent echoed with all the fervour of his heart. She returned into the glare of popularity, but a hope may easily be indulged that the pressure of subsequent relative afflictions and of old age were not permitted to come upon her unaccompanied by the impressions and consolations of true religion. Her elegant biographer, Mr. Campbell, draws a veil p. 80over the state of her mind during her last hours, which it would be deeply interesting to penetrate. Would she not then, if reason were undimmed, reflect upon the faithful counsel she received with Scott's Bible as being of infinitely greater value than the applause of myriads or the fame of ages?'

Beccles, where this good Mr. Sloper lived, and where the writer of this extract was a respectable solicitor—I believe the firm of Rix and Son still exists—was a small market town about eight miles from Wrentham, inland. At that time it ranked as the third town in Suffolk. Towards the west it is skirted by a cliff, once washed by the estuary which separated the eastern portions of Norfolk and Suffolk. There is every reason to believe that ages back the mouth of the Yare was an estuary or arm of the sea, and extended with considerable magnitude for many miles up the country. The herring fishery was thus a principal source of emolument to the inhabitants, and in the time of the Conqueror the fee farm rent of the manor of Beccles to the King was 60,000 herrings, and in the time of the Confessor 20,000. About 956 the manor and advowson of Beccles were granted by King Edwy to the monks of Bury, and remained in p. 81their possession until the dissolution of the religious houses under Henry VIII.

As I have said, and as I repeat, in these languid days—when the old creeds have lost their power and the old bottles are bursting with new wine—the glory of East Anglia was that it was the first to stand up in the face of priest or king for the truth—or what it held to be such. Amongst the early martyrs under Mary were three burnt at Beccles—Thomas Spicer, of Winston, labourer, John Deny, and Edmond Poole. This was in the year 1556. Their crime in the indictment, drawn up by Dr. Hopton, Bishop of Norwich, and his Chancellor, Dunning, according to Fox, was:

'1. First was articulate against them that they belieued not the Pope of Rome to bee supreame head immediately in Christ on earth of the Universall Catholike Church.

'2. That they belieued not holie bread and holie water, ashes, palmes, and all other like ceremonies used in the Church to bee good and laudable for stirring up the people to devotion.

'3. Item that they belieued not afterwards of consecration spoken by the priest, the very naturall body of Christ, and no other substance of bread and wine to bee in the Sacrament of the altar.

p. 82'4. Item that they belieued it to bee idolatry to worship Christ in the Sacrament of the altar.

'5. Item that they tooke bread and wine in remembrance of Christ's Passion.

'6. Item that they would not followe the crosse in procession nor bee confessed to a priest.

'7. Item that they affirmed no mortal man to have in himself free will to do good or evill.'

It appears that the writ had not come down, nevertheless these brave men were burnt at the stake. 'When they came,' continues Fox, 'to the reciting of the creed, Sir John Silliard spake to them, "That is well said, sirs. I am glad to heare you saie you do belieue the Catholike Church; that is the best word I heard of you yet."

'To which his sayings Edmond Poole answered, "Though they belieue the Catholike Church, yet do they not belieue in their Popish Church, which is no part of Christ's Catholike Church, and, therefore, no part of their beliefe."

'When they rose from praier they all went joyfullie to the stake, and, being bound thereto, and the fire burning about them, they praised God in such an audible voice that it was wonderful to all those who stood bye and heard them. Then one Robert Bacon, dwelling in the said Beccles, a p. 83very enemy to God's truth, and a persecutor of His people, being then present, within the hearing thereof willed the tormentors to throwe on faggots to stop the knaues breathes, as he termed them; so hot was his burning charitie. But these good men, not regarding their malice, confessed the truth, and yielded their lives to the death for the testimonie of the same very gloriouslie and joyfullie.'

These men were the precursors of that Nonconformity which has made England the home of the free, and such men abounded in East Anglia. Under Queen Elizabeth they had as bad a time of it almost as under Queen Mary. For instance, we find under Dr. Freke, Bishop of Norwich, and in the reign of glorious Queen Bess, as her admirers term her, Mathew Hammond, a poor ploughwright, of Hethersett, was condemned as a heretic, had his ears cut off, and after the lapse of a week was committed, in the Castle ditch at Norwich, to the more agonizing torment of the flames. The translation of Dr. Whitgift to the See of Canterbury was the signal for augmented rigour. He was charged by his imperious mistress to restore religious uniformity, which she confessed, notwithstanding all her precautions, ran out of square. One of the p. 84first victims to this new *rigime* was William Fleming, Rector of Beccles. The living of Beccles at this period was vested in Lady Anne Gresham, the widow of Sir Thomas Gresham, the founder of the Royal Exchange. Previously to her marriage, she was the widow of William Rede, merchant, of London and Beccles. Under James I. and Bishop Wren, men of integrity and conscience fared worse than under Queen Elizabeth, and naturally the people thus persecuted formed themselves into a Church. That in Beccles dated from 1652, and in the covenant drawn up on the occasion we find it was resolved:

'1. That we will for ever acknowledge and admit the Lord to be our God in Jesus Christ, giving up ourselves to Him to be His people.

'2. That we will alwaies endevour, through the grace of God assisting us, to walke in all His waies and ordinances, according to His written Word, which is the only sufficient rule of good life for every man. Neither will we suffer ourselves to be polluted by any sinful waies, either publike or private, but endeavour to abstaine from the very appearance of evill, giving no offence to the Jew or Gentile, or the Churches of Christ.

'3. That we will humbly and willingly submit p. 85ourselves to the government of Christ in this Church—in the administration of the Word, the seals, and discipline.

'4. That we will in all love approve our communion as brethren by watching over one another, and as such shall be; counsel, administer, relieve, assist, and bear with one another, serving one another in love.

'5. Lastly, we do not covenant or promise these things in our own, but in Christ's strength; neither do we confine ourselves to the words of this covenant, but shall at all time account it our duty to embrace any further light or covenant which shall be revealed to us out of God's Word.'

This covenant, however, was not to prevent in after time censure being cast on others who, endeavouring to preserve its spirit, were led to think differently from the majority. For instance, we find in 1656 two persons, who had been members of the Independent church at Beccles, received adult baptism, and in so doing were considered to have given 'offence' to the church, and were desired to appear and give an account of their practices.

At one time there was little of what we know as congregational singing. In 1657 it was agreed by the Beccles church 'that they do put in p. 86practice the ordinance of singing in the publick upon the forenoon and afternoon of the Lord's daies, and that it be between praier and sermon; and also it was agreed that the New England translation of the Psalmes be made use of by the church at their times of breaking of bread, and it was agreed that the next Lord's day, seventh night, might be the day to enter upon the work of singing in publick.' It is interesting to note that one of the pastors of the Beccles church was a Mr. Nokes, who had been trained—where Calamy and many others were trained—at the University of Utrecht, and that in the same year in which Dr. Watts accepted the pastoral office, he addressed to Mr. Nokes a poem on 'Friendship,' which is still included in the Doctor's works. Dissent, when I was a boy, was considered low. We were contemptuously termed 'pograms,' a term of reproach the origin of which I have never learnt. The landed gentry, the small squires, the lawyers and the doctors, and the tradespeople who pandered to their prejudices and fattened on their patronage, were slow to say a word in favour of a Dissenter. The poor who went to chapel were excluded from many benefits enjoyed by their fellow-parishioners. It was the fashion to treat them with scorn, yet I p. 87have heard one of the most excellent and finished gentlemen in the district declare that he heard better talk in my father's parlour than he did anywhere else in the neighbourhood, and I can well believe it, for the Dissenting minister, as a rule, at that time, was a better read man, and a more studious one, than the clergyman of the district, in spite of his University education; and in matters affecting the welfare of the nation, and that came under the denomination of politics, his views were far more rational than those of Churchmen in general, and the clergy in particular. We learn from Milton's State Papers that the churches of East Anglia petitioned Oliver Cromwell that the three nations might enjoy the blessings of a godly, upright magistracy; that they might have Courts of Judicature in their own country; and that honest men of known fidelity and uprightness might be authorized to determine trivial matters of debt or difference. Assuredly the East Anglian saints—the latter term was, and, strange to say, is still, used as a term of reproach—were wise and right-thinking men where Church government and public policy were concerned. We love to read the story of the Pilgrim Fathers. With what rapture Mrs. Hemans wrote:

> p. 88'What sought they thus afar?
> Bright jewels of the mine?
> The wealth of seas? the spoils of war?
> They sought a faith's pure shrine.
> 'Ay, call it holy ground,
> The soil where first they trod;
> They left unstained what there they found—
> Freedom to worship God.'

But it seems to me that a greater glory was won by, and a greater honour should be paid to, the men who did not cross the Atlantic; who did not seek an asylum in a foreign land; who remained at home to suffer—to die, if need be, to uphold the rights of conscience, and to fight the good fight of faith. It is not even in our tolerant, and, as we deem it, more enlightened day, that full justice is done to these men. In what calls itself good society you meet men and women whose ancestors were Dissenters, and yet who are ashamed of the fact—a fact of which no one can be ashamed who feels how in East Anglia, at any rate, the religious teaching of Dissent purified the life of the people, enlarged their political views, and helped this great land of ours to sweep into a better and a younger day.

p. 89CHAPTER IV.
politics and theology.

Homerton academy — W. Johnson Fox, M.P. — Politics in 1830 — Anti-Corn Law speeches — Wonderful oratory.

About 1830 there was, if not a good deal of actual light let into such dark places as our Suffolk village — where it was considered the whole duty of man, as regards the poor, to attend church and make a bow to their betters (a rustic ceremony generally performed by pulling the lock of hair on the forehead with the right hand), and to be grateful for the wretched station of life in which they were placed — at any rate, a great shaking among the dry bones. One summer morning an awe fell on the parish as it ran from one to another that the guard of the Yarmouth and London Royal Mail had left word with the ostler at the Spread Eagle that George the Fourth was dead; then a certain dull sound as of cannon firing afar off had been wafted across the German Ocean, and had p. 90given rise to mysterious speculations on the subject of Continental wars, in which Suffolk lads might have to ''list' as 'sogers'; and last of all there came that grand excitement when — North and South, East and West — the nation rose as one man to demand political and Parliamentary Reform. It was a delusion, perhaps, that cry, but it was a glorious one, nevertheless; that the millennium could be delayed when we had Parliamentary Reform no one for a moment doubted. The sad but undeniable fact that mostly men are fools with whom beer is omnipotent had not then entered into men's minds, and thus England and Scotland some sixty years ago wore an aspect of activity and enthusiasm of which the present generation can have no idea, and which, perhaps, can never occur again.

Far away in the distant city which the Suffolk villagers called Lunnon, there was a Suffolk lad, whose relations kept a very little shop just by us, who was born at Uggeshall — pronounced Ouchell by the common people — on a very small farm, and who, as Unitarian preacher and newspaper writer, had been and was doing his best in the good cause; but it was not the influence of W. Johnson Fox — for it is of him I write — that did much in our little p. 91village to leaven the mass with the leaven of Reform. While quite a lad the

Foxes went to Norwich, where the future preacher and teacher worked as a weaver boy. In after-years it was often my privilege to meet Mr. Fox, who had then attained no small share of London distinction, amongst whose hearers were men, often many of the most distinguished *literati* of the day—such as Dickens and Forster—and who was actually to sit in Parliament as M.P. for Oldham, where, old as he was—and Mr. Gladstone says, 'People who wish to succeed in Parliament should enter it young'—he occupied a most respectable position, all the more creditable when you remember that Parliament, even at that recent date, was a far more select and aristocratic assembly than any Parliament of our day, or of the future, can possibly be. Mr. Fox had been educated at Homerton Academy—as such places were then termed (college is the word we use now)—under the good and venerable Dr. Pye-Smith, whose 'Scripture Testimony to the Messiah' was supposed to have given Unitarianism a deadly blow, but whom I chiefly remember as a very deaf old man, and one of the first to recognise the fact that the Bible and geology were not necessarily opposed to each other, p. 92and to welcome and proclaim the truth—at that time received with fear and trembling, if received at all—that the God of Nature and the God of Revelation were the same. There was a good deal of free inquiry at Homerton Academy, which, however, Mr. Fox assured me, gradually subsided into the right amount of orthodoxy as the time came for the student to exchange his sure and safe retreat for the fiery ordeal of the deacon and the pew. My father and Johnson Fox had been fellow-students, and for some time corresponded together. The correspondence in due time, however, naturally ceased, as it was chiefly controversial, and nothing can be more irksome than for two people who have made up their minds, and whom nothing can change, to be arguing continually, and the friendship between them in some sense ceased as the one remained firm to, and the other wandered farther and farther from, the modified Calvinism of the Wrentham Church and pulpit, where, as in all orthodox pulpits at that time, it was taught that men were villains by necessity, and fools, as it were, by a Divine thrusting on; that for some a Saviour had been crucified, that there might be a way of escape from the wrath of an angry and unforgiving God; whilst for the p. 93vast mass—to whom the name of Christ had never been made known, to whom the Bible had never been sent—there was an impending doom, the awful horror of which no tongue could tell, no imagination conceive. But to the last Mr. Fox — especially if you met him with his old-fashioned hat on in the street — looked far more of a Puritan divine than of the literary man, or the chief of the advanced thinkers in Church and State, or an M.P. At a later time what pleasure it gave me to listen to this distinguished East Anglian as he appeared at the crowded Anti-Corn Law meetings held in Covent Garden or Drury Lane! Ungainly in figure, monotonous in tone, almost without a particle of action, regarded as free in his religious opinions by the vast majority of his audience, who were, at that time, prone, even in London, to hold that Orthodoxy, like Charity, covered a multitude of sins. What an orator he was! How smoothly the sentences fell from his lips one after the other; with what happy wit did he expose Protectionist fallacies, or enunciate Free Trade principles, which up to that time had been held as the special property of the philosopher, far too subtle to be understood and appreciated by the mob! With what felicity did he illustrate his weighty theme; with p. 94what clearness did he bring home to the people the wrong and injustice done to every one of them by the landlord's attempt to keep up his rent by a tax on corn; and then with what glowing enthusiasm did they wait and listen for the climax, which, if studied, and perhaps artificial, seemed like the ocean wave to grow grander and larger the nearer it came, till it fell with resistless force on all around. It seems to me like a dream, all that distant and almost unrecorded past. I see no such meetings, I hear no such orators now. As Mr. Disraeli said of Lord Salisbury when he was Lord Robert Cecil, there was a want of finish about his style, and the remark holds good of the orator of to-day as contrasted with the platform speaker of the past. It is impossible to fancy anyone in our sober age attempting, to say nothing of succeeding in the attempt (my remarks, of course, do not apply to Irish audiences or Irish orators), to get an audience to rise *en masse* and swear never to fold their arms, never to relax their efforts, till their end was gained and victory won; yet Mr. Fox did so, and long as I live shall I remember the night when, in response to his impassioned appeal, the whole house — and it was crowded to the ceiling — rose, ladies in the boxes, decent City men in the pit, gods in p. 95the gallery — to swear never to tire, never to rest, never to slacken, till the peasant at the plough, the cotton-spinner in the mill, the collier in the mine, the lone widow stitching for life far into the early morning in her wretched garret, and the pauper in his still more wretched cellar, ate their untaxed loaf. As the 'Publicola' of the *Weekly Dispatch*, Mr. Fox laboured to the end of his life in the good cause of Peace, Retrenchment, and Reform. It is not right that his memory should remain unrecorded—his life assuredly was an interesting one. Harriet Martineau writes in her autobiography that 'his editorial correspondence with me was unquestionably the reason, and in great measure the cause, of the greatest intellectual progress I ever made before the age of thirty.'

But it was not from William Johnson Fox that at that time came to our small village the grain of light that was to leaven the lump around. Lecturing and oratory, and even public tea-meetings, were things almost unknown. Now and then a deputation from the London Missionary Society came to Wrentham, and in this way I remember William Ellis, then a missionary from Madagascar, and Mr. George Bennett, who, in conjunction with the Rev. Mr. Tyerman, had been on a tour of p. 96inspection to the islands of the South Seas, and to whose tales of travel rustic audiences listened with delight. Once upon a time—but that was later—the Religious Tract Society sent a deputation in the shape of a well-known travelling secretary, Mr. Jones. This Mr. Jones was inclined to corpulency, and I can well remember how we all laughed when, on one occasion, the daughter of a neighbouring minister, having opened the door in reply to his knock, ran delightedly into her papa's study to announce the arrival of the Tract Society!

A great impression was also made in all parts of the country by the occasional appearances of the Anti-Slavery Society's lecturers. In 1831, as Sir G. Stephen tells us, the younger section of the Anti-Slavery body resolved to stir up the country by sending lecturers to the villages and towns of the country. The M.P.'s did not much like it. The idea was novel to them. 'Trust to Parliament,' said they; the outsiders replied, 'Trust to the people.' This scheme of agitation, however, was rejected, and would have fallen to the ground had not a benevolent Quaker of the name of Cropper come forward. 'Friend S., what money dost thou want?' 'I want #20,000, but I will p. 97begin if I can get one.' 'Then, I will give thee #500.' Joseph Sturge immediately followed with a promise of #250, and Mr. Wilberforce twenty guineas; and #1,000 was raised, and competent agents sent out. It proved by no means an easy matter to obtain these lecturers, for their duty was not confined to lecturing; they had also to revive drooping anti-slavery societies and to establish new ones. Also they were to have collections at the end of every lecture. One of them who came to Wrentham was Captain Pilkington. 'Pilkington,' writes Sir George Stephen, 'was a pleasing lecturer, and won over many by his amiable manners; but he wanted power, and resigned in six months.' We in Wrentham, however, did not think so, and I can to this day recall the sensation he created in our rustic minds as he described the horrors of slavery, and showed us the whip and chains by which those horrors were caused. To the Dissenting chapel most of these lecturers were indebted for their audience, and if I ever worked hard as a boy, it was to get signatures to anti-slavery petitions. Naturally, a Church parson came to regard all that was attacked by Reformers as a bulwark of the Establishment, and in our part the Meetingers' were the sole friends of the slave.

p. 98As was to be expected, the reading of the village was of the most limited description. It is true we children jumped for joy as once a month came the carrier's cart from Beccles, with the books for the club—the *Evangelical Magazine*, for all the principal families of the congregation, and the *Penny Magazine* and *Chambers's Journal*—then but in their infancy—for ourselves; but, apart from that, there was no reading worth mentioning. That which most astonishes the tourist in Ireland is the way in which people read the newspapers. In our Suffolk village the very reverse was the case, partly because there were few newspapers to read, partly because there were few to read them, and partly because they were dear to buy. The one paper which we took in was the *Suffolk Chronicle*, which made its appearance on Saturday morning, the price of which was sixpence, and which was edited by a sturdy Radical of the name of King, who to the last held to the belief that to have a London letter full of literary or critical talk for the Suffolk farmers was, not to put too fine a point on it, to throw pearls before swine. And perhaps he was right. I can well remember, when one of my early poetical contributions appeared in its columns, how a fear was expressed to me by a farmer's widow in p. 99our parish, lest 'it had cost me a lot o' money' to have that effort of my muse in print. Mr. Childs, of Bungay, had many experiences, equally rustic and still more illustrative of the simplicity of the class. Once upon a time one of them came in a great state of excitement for a copy of the 'Life of Mr. General Gazetteer.' On another occasion a farmer's wife came in search of a Testament. She wanted it directly, and she wanted it of a large type. A specimen was selected, which met with the worthy woman's approval. But the question was, could she have it in half an hour, as she would be away for that time shopping in the town, and would call for it on her return. She was told that she could, and great was her astonishment when, on calling on her return for the Testament, there it was, printed in the particular type she had selected, ready for her use.

I have a very strong idea that the calm of the country and the peaceful occupations of the people had not a very rousing influence upon the intellect. I may go further, and say that the cares of the farm, when high farming was unknown, did not much lift at that time the master above the man. The latter wore a smock-frock, while the former, perhaps, sported a blue coat with brass buttons, and had rather a better kind of head-dress, and p. 100ambled along on a little steady cob, that knew at which ale-house to call for the regular allowance, quite as well as his master. But as regards talk—which was chiefly of bullocks and pigs—well, there really was no very great difference after all. To such religion was the mainspring which kept the whole intellect going; and religion was to be had at the meeting. And I can well remember how strange it seemed to me that these rough, simple, untutored sons of the soil could speak of it with enthusiasm, and could pray, at any rate, with astonishing fervour. Away from the influence of the meeting-house there existed a Bœotian state of mind, only to be excited by appeals to the senses of the most palpable character, a state of mind in which faith—the evidence of things not seen, according to Paul—was quite out of the question; and I regret to say that, notwithstanding the activity of the last fifty years and the praiseworthy and laborious efforts of the East Anglian clergy in all quarters, suitably to rouse and feed the intellect of the East Anglian peasantry, a good deal yet remains to be done. Only a year or two ago, riding on an omnibus in a Suffolk village, the driver asked me if people could go to America by land. 'Of course not,' was my reply. 'Why do you ask such a p.

101question?' Well, it came out that he had 'heerd tell how people got to Americay in ten days; and he did not see how they could do that unless they went by land, and had good hosses to get 'em there at that time.' On my explaining the real state of affairs, he admitted, by way of apology, that he was not much of a traveller himself. Once he had been to Colchester; but that was a long time ago.

But to return to the *Suffolk Chronicle*. It was my duty as a lad, when it had been duly studied at home, to take it to the next subscriber, and I fancy by the time the paper had gone its round it was not a little the worse for wear. But there were other political impulses which tended to create and feed the sacred flame of civil and religious liberty. In one corner of the village lived a small shopkeeper, who stored away, among his pots and pans of treacle and sugar and grocery, a few well-thumbed copies, done up in dirty brown paper, of the squibs and caricatures published by Hone, whom I can just remember, a red-faced old gentleman in black, in the *Patriot* office, and George Cruikshank, with whom I was to spend many a merry hour in after-life. This small shopkeeper was one of the chapel people—a kind of superintendent in the Sunday-school, for which office he p. 102was by no means fitted, but there was no one else to take the berth, and as the family also dealt with him in many ways, I had often to repair to his shop. It was then our young eyes were opened as to the wickedness in high places by the perusal of the 'Political House that Jack built,' and other publications of a similar revolutionary character. Nothing is sacred to the caricaturist, and half a century ago bishops and statesmen and lords and kings were very fair subjects for the exercise of his art. In our day things have changed for the better, partly as the result of the Radical efforts, of which respectability at that time stood so much in awe. London newspapers rarely reached so far as Wrentham. It was the fashion then to look to Ipswich for light and leading. However, as the cry for reform increased in strength, and the debates inside the House of Commons and out waxed fiercer, now and then even a London newspaper found its way into our house, and I can well remember how our hearts glowed within us as some one of us read, while father smoked his usual after-dinner pipe, previous to going out to spend the afternoon visiting his sick and afflicted; and how such names as Earl Grey, and Lord John Russell, and Lord Brougham—the people then called him p. 103Harry Brougham; it was a pity that he was ever anything else—were familiar in our mouths as household words.

In another way also there came to the children in Wrentham the growing perception of a larger world than that in which we lived, and moved, and had our being. One of the historic sites of East Anglia is Framlingham, a small market town, lying a little off the highroad to London, a few miles from what always seemed to me the very uninteresting village of Needham Market, though at one time Godwin, the author of 'Caleb Williams,' preached in the chapel there. There is now a public school for Suffolk boys at Framlingham, and it may yet make a noise in the world. Framlingham in our time has given London Mr. Jeaffreson, a successful man of letters, and Sir Henry Thompson, a still more successful surgeon. In my young days it was chiefly noted for its castle. The mother of that amiable and excellent lady, Mrs. Trimmer, also came from Framlingham; and it is to be hoped that the old town may have had something to do with the formation of the character of a woman whom now we should sneer at, perhaps, as goody-goody, but who, when George the Third was King, did much for the education and improvement p. 104of the young. I read in Mrs. Trimmer's life 'that her father was a man of an excellent understanding, and of great piety; and so high was his reputation for knowledge of divinity, and so exemplary his moral conduct, that, as an exception to their general rule, which admitted no laymen, he was chosen member of a clerical club in the town (Ipswich) in which he resided. From him,' continues the biographer of the daughter, 'she imbibed the purest sentiments of religion and virtue, and learnt betimes the fundamental principles of Christianity.' Well, it is hoped Mr. Kirby did his best for his daughter; but, after all, how much more potent is the influence of a mother! And hence I may claim for Framlingham a fair share in the formation of even so burning and shining a light as Mrs. Trimmer.

The name Framlingham, say the learned, or did say—for what learned men say at one time does not always correspond with what they say at another—is composed of two Saxon words, signifying the habitation of strangers; and to strangers the place is still rich in interest. In its church sleeps the unfortunate, but heroic, Earl of Surrey, whose harmonious verse still delights the students of English literature. Some say he was born at p. 105Framlingham. This is matter of doubt; but there is no doubt about the fact that he was buried there by his son, the Earl of Northampton, who erected a handsome monument to his father's memory. The monument is an elevated tomb, with the Earl's arms and those of his lady in the front in the angles, and with an inscription in the centre. It has his effigy in armour, with an ermined mantle, his feet leaning against a lion couchant. On his left is his lady in black, with an ermined mantle and a coronet. Both have their hands held up as in prayer. On a projecting plinth in front is the figure of his second son, the Earl of Northampton, in armour, with a mantle of ermine, kneeling in prayer. Behind, in a similar plinth, kneeling with a coronet, and in robes, is his eldest daughter, Jane, Countess of Westmoreland, on the right; and his third daughter Catherine, the wife of Lord Henry Berkeley on the left. The monument is kept in order, and painted occasionally, as directed by the Earl of Northampton, out of the endowment of his hospital at Greenwich. In repairing the monument in October, 1835, the Rev. George Attwood, curate of Framlingham, discovered the remains of the Earl lying embedded in clay, directly under his figure on his tomb. It is p. 106difficult now to find what high treason the chivalrous and poetic and gallant Earl had been guilty of; but at that time our eighth Henry ruled the land, and if he wished anyone out of the way, he had not far to go for witnesses or judge or jury ready to do his wicked and wanton will. To the shame of England be it said, the Earl of Surrey was beheaded when he was only thirty years of age. No particulars are preserved of his deportment in prison or on the scaffold, but from the noble spirit he evinced at his trial, and from his general character, it cannot be doubted that he behaved in the last scene of his existence with fortitude and dignity. On the barbarous injustice to which he was sacrificed comment is unnecessary; but regret at his early fate is increased by the circumstance that Henry was in extremities when he ordered his execution, and that his swollen and enfeebled hands were unequal to the task of signing his death-warrant. In this respect more fortunate was the father of Surrey, the Duke of Norfolk, who is buried near the altar of the church at Framlingham. He also was condemned to death, but in the meanwhile the King died, and his victim was set free. Not far off is the tomb of Henry Fitzroy, a natural son of King Henry. He p. 107was a friend of Surrey, and was to have married his sister. The other monuments which adorn the interior of this magnificent church are a table of black marble, supported by angels, to the memory of Sir Robert Hitcham, a mural monument by Roubillac, and others to commemorate virtues and graces, as embodied in the lives of decent men and women in whom the world has long ceased to take any interest.

The venerable castle—here I quote Dr. Dugdale's 'British Traveller'—with its eventful history, imparts the strongest interest to the town of Framlingham. Tradition refers its origin to the sixth century, and ascribes it to Redwald, one of the early Saxon monarchs. St. Edmund the Martyr fled hither in 870, and was besieged by the Danes, who took Framlingham and held it fifty years. The Norman King gave the castle to the Bigods. The castle passed through many hands. It was there Queen Mary took shelter when, after the death of Edward VI., Lady Jane Grey was called to the throne, and thence she came to London, on the capture of the former, to take possession of the crown. It was an evil day for England when she came to Framlingham Castle and beguiled the hearts of the Suffolk men. Old p. 108Fox tells us that when Mary had returned to her castle at Framlingham there resorted to her 'the Suffolke men, who, being alwayes forward in promoting the proceedings of the Gospel, promised her their aid and help, so that she would not attempt the alteration of the religion which her brother, King Edward, had before established by laws and orders publickly enacted, and received by the consent of the whole realm in his behalf. She afterwards agreed with such promise made unto them that no innovation should be made of religion, as that no man would or could then have misdoubted her. "Victorious by the aid of the Suffolke men," Queen Mary soon forgot her promise. They of course remonstrated. It was, methinks,' adds Fox, 'an heavie word that she answered to the Suffolke men afterwards which did make supplication unto her grace to performe her promise. "For so much," saith she, "as you being but members desire to rule your head, you shall one day perceive the members must obey their head, and not look to rule over the same."' Well, Queen Mary was as good as her word. As Fox adds, 'What she performed on her part the thing itself and the whole story of the persecution doth testifie.' But the stubborn Suffolk gospellers were p. 109not to be put down, and a remnant had been left in

Framlingham, as well as in other parts of the country. At Framlingham we find a Richard Goltie, son-in-law of Samuel Ward, of Ipswich, was instituted to the rectory in 1630. In 1650 he refused the engagement to submit to the then existing Government, and was removed, when Henry Sampson, M.A., a fellow of Pembroke Hall, Cambridge, was appointed by his college to the vacancy. He continued there till the Restoration, when Mr. Goltie returned and took possession of the living, which he continued to hold till his death. Not being satisfied to conform, Mr. Sampson continued awhile preaching at Framlingham to those who were attached to his ministry, in private houses and other buildings, and by his labours laid the foundation of the Congregational or Independent Church in that town, as appears from a note in the Church Book belonging to the Dissenters meeting at Woodbridge, in the Quay Lane. Mr. Sampson collected materials for a history of Nonconformity, a great part of which is incorporated in Calamy and Palmer's works. It was to him that John Fairfax, of Needham Market, wrote, when he and some other ministers were shut up in Bury Gaol for the crime of preaching the Gospel. p. 110It appears that they had met in the parish church, at Walsham-le-Willows, where, after the liturgy was read by the clergyman of the parish, a sermon was preached by a non-licensed minister. The party were then taken and committed to prison, where they remained till the next Quarter Sessions, when they were released upon their recognisances to appear at the next Assizes. Then, it seems, though not convicted upon any other offence, upon the suggestion of the justices, to whom they were strangers, they were committed again to prison, on the plea that *they were persons dangerous to the public peace.* Thus were Dissenters treated in the good old times. Mr. Sampson seems to have fared somewhat better. After his removal, he travelled on the Continent, returned to London, entered himself at the College of Physicians, and lived and died in good repute. The old congregation having become Unitarian, a new one was formed, and of this Church a pillar was Mr. Henry Thompson—a gentleman well known and widely honoured in his day. This Mr. Thompson had a son, who was sent to Wrentham to be educated for awhile with myself. An uncle of his, one of the most amiable of men, lived at Southwold, close by, and I presume it was by his means that the settlement was p. 111effected. Be that as it may, the change was a welcome one, as it gave me a pleasant companion for nearly five years of boyish life. I confess my two sisters—one of whom has, alas! long been in her grave—did all they could in the way of sports and pastimes to meet my wants and wishes, and act like boys; but the fact is, though it may be doubted in these days of Women's Rights, girls are not boys, nor can they be expected to behave as such.

I confess the advent of this young Thompson from Framlingham was a great event in our small family circle. In the first place he came from a town, and that at once gave him a marked superiority. Then his father kept a horse and gig, for it was thus young Thompson came to Wrentham, and all the world over a gig has been a symbol of the respectability dear to the British heart; and he had been for that time and as an only son carefully and intelligently trained by one of the family who, in the person of the late Edward Miall, founder of the *Nonconformist*, and M.P. for Bradford, was supposed to be the incarnation of what was termed the dissidence of Dissent. Young Thompson was also what would be called a genteel youth, and gave me ideas as to wearing straps to my trousers, oiling my hair, and generally adorning p. 112my person, which had never entered into my unsophisticated head. He also had been to London, and as Framlingham was some twenty miles nearer the Metropolis—the centre of intelligence—than Wrentham, the intelligence of a Framlingham lad was of course expected, ` *fortiori*, to be of a stronger character than that of one born twenty miles farther from the sun of London. There was also a good deal of talent in the family on the mother's side. Mrs. Thompson was a Miss Medley, and Mr. Medley was an artist of great merit, the son of Mr. Medley, of Liverpool, a leading Baptist minister in his day, and a writer of hymns still sung in Baptist churches. Mr. Medley was also active as a Liberal, and was credited by us boys with a personal acquaintance with no less illustrious an individual than the great Brougham himself. Once or twice he came to lodge during the summer at Southwold; naturally he was visited there by his grandson, who would return well primed with political anecdote to our rustic circle, and was deemed by me more of an authority than ever. Once or twice, too, I had the honour of being a visitor, and heard Mr. Medley, a fine old gentleman, who lived to a very advanced age, talk of art and artists and other matters quite out of p. 113my usual sphere. It is not surprising, then, that the grandson became in time quite an artist himself, though he is better known to the world, not so much in that capacity, but as Sir Henry Thompson, certainly not the least distinguished surgeon of our day. In Lord Beaconsfield's last novel, 'Endymion,' we have a passing reference to one Wrentham lad, Sir Charles Wetherell, as 'the eccentric and too uncompromising Wetherell.' Assuredly the fame of another lad, Sir Henry Thompson, connected with Wrentham, will longer live.

This reference to Sir Henry Thompson reminds me of his early attempts at rhyme, which I trust he will forgive me for rescuing from oblivion. Once upon a time we captured a young cuckoo, and having carefully gorged it with bread-and-milk, and left it in a nest in an outhouse, which we devoted mainly to rabbits, the next morning the poor bird was found to be dead. A prize was offered for the best couplet. Three of us contended. My sister wrote:

> 'This lonely sepulchre contains
> A little cuckoo's dead remains.'

I wrote:

> 'To our grief, cuckoo sweet
> Is lying underneath our feet.'

p. 114Thompson took quite a different and, read by the light of his subsequent career, a far more characteristic view of the case. He took care, as a medical man, to dwell on the cause which had terminated the career of so interesting a bird. According to him,

> 'It had a breast as soft as silk,
> And died of eating bread-and-milk.'

Assuredly in this case the child was father to the man.

But the great awakening of the time, that which made the dry bones live, and fluttered the dove-cotes of Toryism—we never heard the word Conservative then—was the General Election. At that time we were always having General Elections. We had one, of course, when George IV. died and King William reigned in his stead; we had another when the Duke was out and the Whigs came in; and then we had another when the cry ran through the land, and reached even the most remote villages of East Anglia, of 'The Bill, the whole Bill, and nothing but the Bill!' Voters were brought down, or up, as the case might be, from all quarters of the land. Coachesfull came tearing along, gorgeous with election flags, and placarded all over with names of rival candidates. p. 115Gentlemen of ancient lineage called to request of the meanest elector the favour of his vote and influence. It was with pain the Liberals of our little village resolved to vote against our Benacre neighbour, Sir Thomas Gooch, who had long represented the county, but of whom the Radicals spoke derisively as Gaffer Gooch, or the Benacre Bull, and chose in his stead a country squire known as Robert Newton Shaw, utterly unknown in our quarter of the county.

It was rather a trying time for the Wrentham Liberals and Dissenters to do their duty, for Sir Thomas was a neighbour, and always was a pleasant gentleman in the parish, and had power to do anyone mischief who went against him. Our medical man did not vote at all. Our squire actually, I believe, supported Sir Thomas, and altogether respectable people found themselves in an extremely awkward position. At Southwold the people were a little more independent, for Gaffer Gooch rarely illuminated that little town with his presence; and as my father, with the economy which is part and parcel of the Scotchman as he leaves his native land, but which rarely extends to his children, had, by teaching gentlemen's sons and other ways, been able to save a p. 116little, which little had been devoted to the purchase of cottage property in Southwold (well do I remember the difficulty there was in collecting the rents; never, assuredly, were people so much afflicted or so unfortunate when the time of payment came), it was for Southwold that he claimed his vote. I, as the son, was permitted to share in the glories of that eventful day. The election took place at school-time, and my companion was Henry Thompson. We had to walk betimes to Frostenden, where Farmer Downing lived, who was that *rara avis* a Liberal tenant farmer; but of course he did not vote tenant farmer, but as a freeholder. It was with alarm that Mrs. Downing saw her lord and master drive off with us two lads in the gig. There had been riots at London, riots as near as Ipswich, and why not at Halesworth? A mile or two after we had started we met, per arrangement, the Southwold contingent, who joined us with flags flying and a band playing, and all the pride and pomp and circumstance of war. We rode in a gig, and our animal was a steady-going mare, and behaved as such; but all had not gigs or steady-going mares. Some were in carts, some were on horseback, some in ancient vehicles furbished up for the occasion; p. 117and as the band played and the people shouted, some of the animals felt induced to dance, and especially was this restlessness on the part of the quadrupeds increased as we neared Halesworth, in the market-place of which was the polling-booth, and in the streets of which we out-lying voters riding in procession made quite a show. Halesworth, or Holser, as it was called, was distant about nine miles, lying to the left of Yoxford, a village which its admirers were wont to call the Garden of Suffolk. In 1809 the Bishop of Norwich wrote from Halesworth: 'The church in this place is uncommonly fine, and the ruins of an old castle (formerly the seat of the Howards) are striking and majestic.' But when we went there the ruins were gone—the more is the pity—and the church remained, at that time held by no less a Liberal than Richard Whately, afterwards Archbishop of Dublin. I used at times to meet with a country gentleman—a brother of a noble lord—who after he had spent a fortune merrily, as country gentlemen did in the good old times, came to live on a small annuity, and, in spite of his enormous daily consumption of London porter at the leading inn of the town, managed to reach a good old age. The hon. gentleman and I were on p. 118friendly terms, and sometimes he would talk of Whately, who had often been at his house. But, alas! he remembered nothing of a man who became so celebrated in his day except that he would eat after dinner any number of oranges, and was so fond of active exercise that he would take a pitchfork and fill his tumbrels with manure, or work just like a labourer on a farm. Of the Doctor's aversion to church-bell ringing we have a curious illustration in a letter which appeared in the *Suffolk Chronicle* in 1825: 'A short time since a wedding took place in the families of two of the oldest and most respectable inhabitants of the town, when it was understood that the Rector had, for the first time since his induction to his living, given permission for the bells to greet the happy pair. After, however, sounding a merry peal a short hour and a half, a message was received at the belfry that the Rector thought they had rung long enough. The tardiness with which this mandate was obeyed soon brought the rev. gentleman in person to enforce his order, which was then reluctantly complied with to the great disappointment of the inhabitants, and mortification of the ringers, several of whom had come from a considerable distance to assist in the festivities of the day.' p. 119The Independent chapel was an old-fashioned meeting-house, full of heavy pillars, which, as they intercepted the view of the preacher, were favourable to that gentle sleep so peculiarly refreshing on a Sunday afternoon—especially in hot weather—in the square and commodious family pew. The minister was an old and venerable-looking divine of the name of Dennant, who was always writing little poems—I remember the opening lines of one,

'A while ago when I was nought,
And neither body, soul, nor thought' —

and whose 'Soul Prosperity,' a volume of sober prose, reached a second edition. His grandson, Mr. J. R. Robinson, now the energetic manager of the *Daily News*, may be said to have achieved a position in the world of London of which his simple-hearted and deeply-devotional grandfather could never have dreamed. As I was the son of a brother minister, Mr. Dennant's house was open to myself and Thompson, though we did not go there on the particular day of which I write. The leading tradesman of the town was a Liberal, and had at least one pretty daughter, and there we went. Most of the day, however, we mixed with the mob which crowded round, while the voters— p. 120you may be sure, not all of them sober—were brought up to vote. The excitement was immense; there was the hourly publication of the state of the poll—more or less unreliable, but, nevertheless, exciting; and what a tumult there was as one or other of the rival candidates drove up to his temporary quarters in a carriage and pair, or carriage and four, made a short speech, which was cheered by his friends and howled at derisively by his foes, while the horses were being changed, and then drove off at a gallop to make the same display and to undergo the same ordeal elsewhere! To be sure, there was a little rough play; now and then a rush was made by nobody in particular, and for no particular reason; or, again, an indiscreet voter—rendered additionally so by indulgence in beer—gave occasion for offence; but really, beyond a scrimmage, a hat broken, a coat or two torn or bespattered with mud, a cockade rudely snatched from the wearer, little harm was done. The voters knew each other, and had come to vote, and had stayed to see the fun. For the timid, the infirm, the old, the day was a trying one; but there was an excitement and a life about the affair one misses now that the ballot has come into play, and has made the voter less of a man than ever. Of course p. 121the shops were shut up. All who could afford to do so kept open house, and at every available window were the bright, beaming faces of the Suffolk fair—oh, they were jolly, those election days of old! Well, in East Anglia, as elsewhere, spite of the parsons, spite of the landlords, spite of the slavery of old custom, spite of old traditions, the freeholders voted Reform, and Reform was won, and everyone believed that the kingdom of heaven was at hand. In ten years, I heard people say, there would be no tithes for the farmer to pay, and welcome was the announcement; for then, as now, the agricultural interest was depressed, and the farmer was a ruined man. Now one takes but a languid interest in the word Reform, but then it stirred the hearts of the people; and how they celebrated their victory, how they hoisted flags and got up processions and made speeches, and feasted and hurrahed, 'twere tedious to tell. All over the land the people rejoiced with exceeding joy. Old things, they believed, had passed away—all things had become new.

p. 122CHAPTER V.
bungay and its people.

Bungay Nonconformity—Hannah More—The Childses—The Queen's Librarian—Prince Albert.

In the beginning of the present century, a disgraceful attack on Methodism—by which the writer means Dissent in all its branches—appeared in what was then the leading critical journal of the age, the *Edinburgh Review*. 'The sources,' said the writer, a clergyman (to his shame be it recorded) of the Church of England—no less distinguished a divine than the far-famed Sydney Smith—'from which we shall derive our extracts are the Evangelical and Methodistical magazines for the year 1807, works which are said to be circulated to the amount of 18,000 or 20,000 every month, and which contain the sentiments of Arminian and Calvinistic Methodists, and of the Evangelical clergymen of the Church of England. We shall use the general term of Methodism to designate these three p. 123classes of fanatics, not troubling ourselves to point out the finer shades and nicer discriminations of lunacy, but treating them as all in one general conspiracy against common-sense and rational orthodox Christianity.' To East Anglia came the reputed worthy Canon for an illustration of what he termed their policy to have a great change of ministers. Accordingly, he reprints from the *Evangelical Magazine* the following notice of an East Anglian Nonconformist ordination, which, by-the-bye, in no degree affects the charge unjustly laid at the door of these 'fanatics,' as engaged 'in one general conspiracy against common-sense and rational orthodox Christianity.' 'Same day the Rev. W. Haward, from Hoxton Academy, was ordained over the Independent Church at Rendham, Suffolk; Mr. Pickles, of Walpole, began with prayer and reading; Mr. Price, of Woodbridge, delivered the introductory discourse, and asked the questions; Mr. Dennant, of Halesworth, offered the ordinary prayer; *Mr. Shufflebottom* [the italics are the Canon's], of Bungay, gave the charge from Acts xx. 28; Mr. Vincent, of Deal, the general prayer; and Mr. Walford, of Yarmouth, preached to the people from Phil. ii. 16.' As a lad, I saw a good deal of Bungay, though I never knew the Shufflebottom p. 124whose name seems to have been such a stumbling-block and cause of offence to the Reverend Canon of St. Paul's. I say Reverend Canon of St. Paul's, because, though the writer had not gained that honour when the review appeared, it was as Canon he returned to the charge when he sanctioned the republication of it in his collected works. It was at Bungay that I had my first painful experience of the utter depravity of the human heart—a truth of which, perhaps, for a boy, I learned too much from the pulpit. The river Waveney runs through Bungay, and one day, fishing there, I lent a redcoat—with whom, like most boys, I was proud to scrape an acquaintance—my line, he promising to return it when I came back from dinner. When I did so, alas! the red-coat was gone.

Nonconformity in Bungay seems to have originated in the days of the Lord Protector, in the person of Zephaniah Smith, who was the author of: (1) 'The Dome of Heretiques; or, a discovery of subtle Foxes who were tyed tayle to tayle, and crept into the Church to do mischief'; (2) 'The Malignant's Plot; or, the Conspiracie of the Wicked against the Just, laid open in a sermon preached at Eyke, in Suffolk, January 23, 1697. Preached and published to set forth the grounds p. 125why the Wicked lay such crimes to the charge of God's people as they are cleare off'; (3) 'The Skillful Teacher.' Beloe says of this Smith that 'he was a most singular character, and among the first founders of the sect of the Antinomians.' One of the first leaders of this sect is said by Wood to have been John Eaton, who was a minister and preacher at Wickham Market, in which situation and capacity Smith succeeded him. This Smith published many other tracts and sermons, chiefly fanatical and with fantastical titles. One is described by Wood, and is called 'Directions for Seekers and Expectants, or a Guide for Weak Christians in these discontented times.' 'I shall not give an extract from these sermons,' writes Beloe, who is clearly, like Wood, by no means a sympathetic or appreciative critic, 'though very curious, but they are not characterized by any peculiarity of diction, and are chiefly remarkable for the enthusiasm with which the doctrine of the sect to which the preacher belonged is asserted and vindicated. The hearers also must have been endowed with an extraordinary degree of patience, as they are spun out to a great length.' Mr. Smith's ministry at Bungay led to a contention, which resulted in an appeal to the young Protector,

Richard Cromwell. p. 126Then we find Mr. Samuel Malbon silenced by the Act of Uniformity, who is described as a man mighty in the Scriptures, who became pastor to the church in Amsterdam. In 1695 we hear of a conventicle in Bungay, with a preacher with a regularly paid stipend of #40 a year. Till 1700 the congregation worshipped in a barn; but in that year the old meeting-house was built, and let to the congregation at #10 per annum. In 1729 it was made over to the Presbyterians or Independents worshipping there, 'for ever.' The founders of that conventicle seem to have suffered for their faith; yet the glorious Revolution of 1688 had been achieved, and William of Orange—who had come from a land which had nobly sheltered the earlier Nonconformists—was seated on the throne.

Bungay, till Sydney Smith made it famous, was not much known to the general public. It was on the borders of the county and out of the way. The only coach that ran through it, I can remember, was a small one that ran from Norwich through Beccles and Bungay to Yarmouth; and, if I remember aright, on alternate days. There was, at any rate, no direct communication between it and London. Bungay is a well-built market town, skirted on the east and west by the navigable river Waveney, p. 127which divides it from Norfolk, and was at one time noted for the manufacture of knitted worsted stockings and Suffolk hempen cloth; but those trades are now obsolete. The great Roger Bigod—one of the men who really did come over with the Conqueror—built its castle, the ruins of which yet remain, on a bold eminence on the river Waveney. 'The castle,' writes Dugdale, 'once the residence and stronghold of the Bigods, and by one of them conceived to be impregnable, has become the habitation of helpless poverty, many miserable hovels having been reared against its walls for the accommodation of the lowest class.' The form of the castle appears to have been octangular. The ruins of two round fortal towers and fortresses of the west and south-west angles are still standing, as also three sides of the great tower or keep, the walls of which are from 7 to 11 feet thick and from 15 to 17 feet high. In the midst of the ruins, on what is called the Terrace, is a mineral spring, now disused, and near it is a vault, or dungeon, of considerable depth. Detached portions of the wall and their foundations are spread in all directions in the castle grounds, a ridge of which, about 40 yards long, forms the southern boundary of a bowling-green which commands delightful prospects. p. 128The mounds of earth raised for the defence of the castle still retain much of their original character, though considerably reduced in height. One of them, facing the south, was partly removed in 1840, with the intention of forming a cattle market. As a boy I often heard of the proud boast of Hugh Bigod, second Earl, one of King Stephen's most formidable opponents, as recorded by Camden:

> 'Were I in my castle of Bungay,
> Upon the river Waveney,
> I would not care for the King of Cockeney.'

In ancient times the Waveney was a much broader stream than it is now, and Bungay was called *Le Bon Eye*, or the good island, then being nearly surrounded by water. Hence the name, in the vulgar dialect, of Bungay. To 'go to Bungay to get a new bottom' was a common saying in Suffolk.

In 1777 we find Hannah More writing to Garrick from Bungay, which she describes as 'a much better town than I expected, very clean and pleasant.' 'You are the favourite bard of Bungay'—at that time the tragedians of the city of Norwich were staying there— 'and,' writes Hannah, who at that time had not become serious and renounced the gaieties of the great world, 'the p. 129dramatic furore rages terribly among the people, the more so, I presume, from being allowed to vent itself so seldom. Everybody goes to the play every night,—that is, every other night, which is as often as they perform. Visiting, drinking, and even card-playing, is for this happy month suspended; nay, I question if, like Lent, it does not stop the celebration of weddings, for I do not believe there is a damsel in the town who would spare the time to be married during this rarely-occurring scene of festivity. It must be confessed, however, the good folks have no bad taste.' It must be recollected that Hannah More in reality belongs to East Anglia. She was the daughter of Jacob More, who was descended from a respectable family at Harleston. He was a High Churchman, but all his family were Nonconformists. His mother used to tell young people that they would have known how to value Gospel privileges had they lived like her, when at midnight pious worshippers went with stealthy steps through the snow to hear the words of inspiration delivered by a holy man at her father's house; while her father, with a drawn sword, guarded the entrance from violent or profane intrusion, adding that they boarded the minister and kept his horse for #10 a year. An unfortunate p. 130lawsuit deprived the Mores of their property, and thus it was that the celebrated Hannah was born at Gloucestershire, and not in Suffolk or Norfolk. The family mansion was at Wenhaston, not very far from Wrentham.

In my young days Bungay owed all its fame and most of its wealth to the far-famed John Childs, who was one of our first Church Rate martyrs, to whom is due mainly the destruction of the Bible-printing monopoly, and to whom the late Edward Miall was much indebted for establishing the *Nonconformist* newspaper. For many years it was the habit of Mr. Childs to celebrate that event by a dinner, at which the wine was good and the talk was better. Old John Childs, of Bungay, had a cellar of port which a dean might have envied; and many was the bottle that I cracked with him as a young man, after a walk from Wrentham to Bungay, a distance of fourteen miles, to talk with him on things in general, and politics in particular. He was emphatically a self-made man—a man who would have made his way anywhere, and a man who had a large acquaintance with the reformers of his day in all parts of the country. On one occasion the great Dan O'Connell came to pay him a visit, much to the delight of the Suffolk Radicals, p. 131and to the horror of the Tories. The first great dinner at which I had the honour of being present, and to which I was taken by my father, who was a great friend of Mr. Childs, was on the occasion of the presentation to the latter of a testimonial by a deputation of distinguished Dissenters from Ipswich in connection with his incarceration in the county gaol at Ipswich, for having refused to pay rates for the support of a Church in which he did not believe, and for the performance of a service in which he took no part. At that time 'the dear old Church of England,' while it was compelled to tolerate Dissent, insisted on Dissent being taxed to the uttermost farthing; and that it does not do so now, and that it is more popular in consequence, is due to the firm stand taken by such men as John Childs of Bungay. He was a great phrenologist. In his garden he had a summer-house, which he facetiously termed his scullery, where he had some three hundred plaster casts, many of which he had taken himself of public individuals and friends and acquaintances. My father was honoured in this way, as also my eldest sister. Sir Henry Thompson and I escaped that honour, but I have not forgotten his dark, piercing glance at our heads, when, as boys, we first came into his presence, and how I p. 132trusted that the verdict was satisfactory. Of course the Childses went to Meeting, but when I knew Bungay Mr. Shufflebottom had been gathered to his fathers, and the Rev. John Blaikie, a Scotchman, and therefore always a welcome guest at Wrentham, reigned in his stead. Mr. Childs had a large and promising family, few of whom now remain. His daughter was an exceptionally gifted and glorious creature, as in that early day it seemed to me. She also died early, leaving but one son, Mr. Crisp, a partner in the well-known legal firm of Messrs. Ashurst, Morris, and Crisp. It was in the little box by the window of the London Coffee House — now, alas! no more — where Mr. Childs, on the occasion of his frequent visits to London, always gathered around him his friends, that I first made the acquaintance of Mr. Ashurst, the head of the firm — a self-made man, like Mr. Childs, of wonderful acuteness and great public spirit. In religion Mr. Ashurst was far more advanced than the Bungay printer. 'It is not a thing to reason about,' said the latter; and so to the last he remained orthodox, attended the Bungay Meeting-house, invited the divines of that order to his house, put in appearance at ordination services, and openings of chapels, and was to be seen at May p. 133Meetings when in town, where occasionally his criticisms were of a freer order than is usually met with at such places.

'The Bungay Press,' wrote a correspondent of the *Bookseller*, on the death of Mr. Charles Childs, who had succeeded his father in the business, 'has been long known for its careful and excellent work. Established some short time before the commencement of the present century, its founder had, for twenty years, limited its productions to serial publications and books of a popular and useful character, and in the year 1823, soon after Mr. John Childs had taken control of the business, upwards of twenty wooden presses were working, at long hours, to supply the rapidly-increasing demand for such works as folio Bibles, universal histories, domestic medicine books, and other publications then issuing in one and two shilling numbers from the press.' Originally Mr. Childs had been in a grocer's shop at Norwich. There he was met with by a Mr. Brightley, a printer and publisher, who, originally a schoolmaster at Beccles, had suggested to young Childs that he had better come and help him at Bungay than waste his time behind a counter. Fortunately for them both the young man acceded to the proposal, and travelled all over p. 134England driving tandem, and doing everywhere what we should now call a roaring trade. Then he married Mr. Brightley's daughter, and became a partner in the firm, which was known as that of John and R. Childs, and, latterly of Childs and Son. 'Uncle Robert,' as I used to hear him called, was little known out of the Bungay circle. He had a nice house, and lived comfortably, marrying, after a long courtship, the only one of the Stricklands who was not a writer. Agnes was often a visitor at Bungay, and not a little shocked at the atrocious after-dinner talk of the Bungay Radicals. 'Do you not think,' said she, in her somewhat stilted and tragic style of talk, one day, to a literary man who was seated next her, author of a French dictionary which the Childses were printing at the time—'Do you not think it was a cruel and wicked act to murder the sainted and unfortunate Charles I.?' 'Why, ma'am,' stuttered the author, while the dinner-party were silent, 'I'd have p-p-poisoned him.' The gifted authoress talked no more that day. Naturally, as a lad, seeing so much of Bungay, I wished to be a printer, but Mr. Childs said there was no use in being a printer without plenty of capital, and so that idea was renounced.

p. 135But to return to Mr. John Childs. About the year 1826, in association with the late Joseph Ogle Robinson, he projected and commenced the publication of a series of books known in the trade as the 'Imperial Edition of Standard Authors,' which for many years maintained an extensive sale, and certainly then met an admitted literary want, furnishing the student and critical reader, in a cheap and handsome form, with dictionaries, histories, commentaries, biographies, and miscellaneous literature of acknowledged value and importance, such as Burke's works, Gibbon's 'Decline and Fall,' Howe's works, the writings of Lord Bacon—books which are still in the market, and which, if I may speak from a pretty wide acquaintance with students' libraries fifty years ago, were in great demand at that time. The disadvantage of such a series is that the books are too big to put in the pocket or to hold in the hand. But I do not know that that is a great disadvantage to a real student who takes up a book to master its contents, and not merely to pass away his time. To study properly a man must be in his study. In that particular apartment he is bound to have a table, and if you place a book on a table to read, it matters little the size of the page, or the number p. 136of columns each page contains. Mr. Childs set the fashion of reprinting standard authors on a good-sized page, with a couple of columns on each page. That fashion was followed by Mr. W. Smith—a Fleet Street publisher, than whom a better man never lived—and by Messrs. Chambers; but now it seems quite to have passed away. On the failure of Mr. Robinson, Mr. Childs' valuable reprints were placed in the hands of Westley and Davis, and subsequently with Ball, Arnold, and Co.; and latterly, I think, the late Mr. H. G. Bohn reissued them at intervals. As to his part publications, when Mr. Childs had given up pushing them, he disposed of them all to Mr. Virtue, of Ivy Lane, Paternoster Row, who then secured almost a monopoly of the part-number trade, and thus made a large fortune. 'I love books that come out in numbers,' says Lord Montford in 'Endymion,' 'as there is a little suspense, and you cannot deprive yourself of all interest by glancing at the last part of the last volume.' And so I suppose in the same way there will always be a part-number trade, though the reapers in the field are many, and the harvest is not what it was.

Active and fiery in body and soul, Mr. John Childs, at a somewhat later period, with the p. 137sympathy and advocacy of Mr. Joseph Hume and other members of Parliament, and aided to a large extent by Lord Brougham, succeeded in procuring the appointment of a Committee of the House of Commons to inquire into the existing King's Printers' Patent for printing Bibles and Acts of Parliament, the period for the renewal of which was near at hand. The principle upon which the patent was originally granted appeared to be *correctness secured only by protection*—a fallacy which the voluminous evidence of the Committee most completely exposed. The late Alderman Besley, a typefounder, and a great friend of John Childs, as well as Robert Childs, practical printers, gave conclusive evidence on this head, and the result was that, although the patent was renewed for thirty years, instead of sixty as before, the Scriptures were sold to the public at a greatly reduced price, and the trade in Bibles, though nominally protected, has ever since been practically free.

Nor did Mr. Childs' labours end here. In Scotland the right of printing Bibles had been granted exclusively to a company of private persons, Blaire and Bruce, neither of whom had any practical knowledge of the art of printing, or took any p. 138interest in the different editions of the Bible. The same men also had the supplying all the public revenue offices of Government with stationery, by which means they enjoyed an annual profit of more than #6,000 a year. When the Government, in an economical mood, ordered them to relinquish the latter contract, not only were they compensated for the loss, but were continued in their vested rights as regards Bible-printing. In Scotland there was no one to interfere with their rights. In England patents had been given not only to the firm of Messrs. Strahan, Eyre and Spottiswoode, but to each of the two Universities of Cambridge and Oxford. Up to 1821 the Bibles of the English monopolists came freely into Scotland, but then a prohibition, supported by decisions in the Court of Sessions and the House of Lords, was obtained. In 1824 Dr. Adam Thompson, of Coldstream, and three ministers were summoned to answer for the high crime and misdemeanour of having, as directors of Bible societies, delivered copies of an edition of Scriptures which had been printed in England, but which the Scotch monopolists would not permit to circulate in Scotland. Bible societies in Scotland had received, in return for their subscription to the London society, copies p. 139of an octavo Bible in large type, to which the Scotch patentees had no corresponding edition, and which was much prized by the aged. And it was because Dr. Thompson and others helped to circulate it, as agents of the London Bible Society, that they were proceeded against. The Scotch Bible, in consequence of the monopoly, was as badly printed as the English one. In order to show how monopoly had failed to secure good work, a gentleman sent to the Archbishop of Canterbury an enormous list of errors which he had found in the Oxford Nonpareil Bible. In an old Scotch edition the apostle is made to say, 'Know ye not that the righteous shall *not* inherit the kingdom of God?' In another edition 'The four beasts of the Apocalypse' are '*sour* beasts.' Dr. Lee, afterwards Principal of Edinburgh University, felt deeply the injustice done by the monopoly, and the heavy taxation consequently imposed upon the British and Foreign Bible Society; but he was a man of the study rather than of the street. Yet in 1837 the monopoly, powerfully defended as it was by Sir Robert Inglis, who dreaded cheap editions of the Word of God, as necessarily incorrect and leading to wickedness and infidelity of all kinds, fell, and it was to John Childs, of p. 140Bungay, that in a great measure the fall was due, while owing to the repeated labours of Dr. Adam Thompson and others, we got cheaper Bibles and Testaments on the other side of the Tweed.

If you turn to the life of Dr. Adam Thompson, of Coldstream, the man who had the most publicly to do with the fall of the monopoly, there can be no doubt on this head. Though specially interested in the English patents, Mr. Childs was aware that the one for Scotland fell, to be renewed sooner by twenty years, and he kept dunning Joseph Hume on the subject, who, Radical Reformer, at that time had his hands pretty full. Mr. Childs had got so far as to have his Committee, and to get the evidence printed. What was the next step? Dr. Thompson's biographer shall tell us. 'Mr. Childs had been looking out for a Scottish Dissenting minister of proved ability, zeal, and influence, who should feel the immense and urgent importance of the question, and after mastering the unjust principles and the injurious results of the monopoly, should testify to these before the Committee, in a weighty and pointed manner, and effectively bring them also before the ministers and people of Scotland. He fixed upon Dr. Thompson, and the letter in which he wrote to the Doctor to prepare p. 141for becoming a witness was the beginning of a ten years' copious correspondence, the first in a series of many hundreds of very lengthy letters, in which Mr. Childs, with great shrewdness, sagacity, and vigour, and with perfect confidence of always being in the right, acted as universal censor, pronouncing oracularly upon all ecclesiastical and political men and organs, expressing unqualified contempt for the House of Lords, and very small satisfaction with the House of Commons, showing no mercy to Churchmen, and little but asperity to Dissenters, and denouncing all British journals as base or blind except the *Nonconformist*.' Only two of these letters are published in Dr. Thompson's biography. I give one, partly because it is interesting, and partly because it is characteristic. Unfortunately, of all John Childs' letters to myself, written in a fine, bold hand, exactly reproduced by his son and grandson, so that I could never tell one from the other, I have preserved none. Childs thus wrote to Dr. Thompson, July 15th, 1839:

'My dear Friend,

'You will be happy to know that I went into Newgate this morning with my friend Ashurst, and heard their pardon read to the Canadians. p. 142They were released this afternoon, and Mr. Parker and Mr. Wixon have been dining with me, and are gone to a lodging, taken for them by Mr. A., where they may remain till their departure on Wednesday. I have just sent to Mr. Tidman to inform him they will worship God and return thanks in his place to-morrow, if all be well. How wonderfully God has appeared for these people! My dear friend, when I first saw them in January all things appeared to be against them, but all has been overruled for good.

'At the time you left on Monday evening, Lord John was making known to the House of Commons, in your own words, the plan proposed by yourself, and adopted by him, to my amazement. Most heartily do I congratulate you on the termination of the event, so decidedly honourable to yourself in every way. I do not expect you will approve of all that I have done, but I felt it to be my duty to address a letter to the *Pilot* on the subject, calling attention to the liberty taken with you, and the manner in which you were humbugged when in concert with the London societies, and the absolute triumph of your cause when conducted with single-handed integrity, intelligence, and energy. If it shall happen that you do not approve of all I have p. 143said, I am sure you ought, because without you, and with you, if you had left it to the fellows here, Scotland's Dissenters would have now appeared the degraded things which, on the

Bible subject, the English Dissenters have appeared in my eyes for some years past. It is due to you. I was fairly rejoiced when I saw Lord John's declaration, because I could see from his answer to Sir James Graham that he meant the thing should be done. Scotland ought to have a day of rejoicing and thanksgiving, and as I said to a friend to whom I wrote in Edinburgh, "You ought to have a monument—the Thompson monument." "That, sir," the guide would say, "is erected to honour a man by whose honest energy and zeal Scotland was freed from the most degrading tyranny—that of a monopoly in printing the Word of God." The tablet should bear that memorable sentence of yours on the first day of your examination, "All monopolies are bad." Of all monopolies religious monopolies are the worst, and of all religious monopolies a monopoly of the Word of God is the most outrageous.' Alas! I have heard nothing of the Thompson monument.

Such a man was John Childs. One more busy p. 144in body and brain I never knew. That he was disposed to be cynical was natural. Most men who see much of the world, and who do not wear coloured glasses, are so. Take the history of the Bible monopoly. The work of its abolition was commenced by John Childs, of Bungay, carried on and completed as far as Scotland was concerned by Dr. Adam Thompson, while the British public in its usual silliness awarded #3,000 to Dr. Campbell, on the plea—I quote the words of the late Dr. Morton Brown, of Cheltenham—that, 'God gave the honour very largely to our friend, Dr. Campbell, to smite this bloated enemy of God and man full in the forehead.' The bloated enemy, as regards Scotland, was dead before Dr. Campbell had ever penned a line. As regards England, I believe it still exists.

It must have been about 1837 that the name of John Childs, of Bungay, was made specially notorious by reason of his refusal to pay Church-rates, and when he had the honour of being the first person imprisoned for their non-payment. He was proceeded against in the Ecclesiastical Courts, and as his refusal to pay was solely on conscientious grounds, he did not contest the matter. The result was, he was sent to Ipswich Gaol for the non-payment p. 145of a rate of 17s. 6d., the animus of the ecclesiastical authorities being manifested by the endorsement of the writ, 'Take no bail.' It was the first death-blow to Church-rates. The local excitement it created was intense and unparalleled. In the House of Commons Sir William Foulkes presented several petitions from Norfolk, and Mr. Joseph Hume several from Suffolk, on the subject. One entire sitting of the House of Commons was devoted to the Bungay Martyr, as Sir Robert Peel ironically termed him. The Bungay Martyr had however, right on his side. It was found that a blot had been hit, and it had to be removed.

The excitement produced by putting Mr. Childs into gaol was intense at that time all over the land. 'I beg to inform you,' wrote a Halesworth Dissenter, Mr. William Lincoln, to the editor of the *Patriot*, at that time the organ of Dissent, 'that my highly-esteemed and talented friend, Mr. John Childs, of Bungay, has just passed through this town, in custody of a sheriff's officer, on his way to our county gaol, by virtue of an attachment, at the suit of Messrs. Bobbet and Scott, churchwardens of Bungay, for non-payment of 17s. 6d. demanded of him as a Church-rate, and subsequent refusal to obey a citation for appearance p. 146at the Bishop's Court.' Naturally the writer remarked: 'It will soon be seen whether proceedings so well in harmony with the days of fire and faggot are to be tolerated in this advanced period of the nineteenth century.' When, in due time, Mr. Childs obtained his release, the event was celebrated at Bungay in fitting style. I find in a private diary the following note: 'This day week was a grand day at Bungay. I heard there were not less than six or seven thousand people there to welcome his return, and the request of the police, that the greatest order might be observed, was fully acted up to. Miss C. did not enter Bungay with her father. I suppose when she found so great a multitude of horsemen, gigs, pedestrians and banners, they thought it better for the young lady and the younger children to retire to the close carriages. Mr. C. during his imprisonment had letters from all parts of the kingdom.' I remember the leading Dissenters came to Bungay with a piece of plate, to present to Mr. Childs, to commemorate his heroism. A dinner was given by Mr. Childs in connection with the presentation.

At that dinner, lad as I was, I was permitted to be present. I had never seen anything so grand or stately before; and that p. 147was my first interview with John Childs, a dark, restless, eagle-eyed man, whom I was to know better and love more for many a long day. I took to Radical writing, and nothing could have pleased John Childs better. I owed much to his friendship in after-life.

In 1833 the Church-rate question was originally raised in Bungay, and many of the Dissenters refused to pay. The local authorities at once took high ground, and put twelve of the recusants into the Ecclesiastical Court. They caved in, leaving to John Childs the honour of martyrdom. At the time of Mr. Childs' imprisonment he had recently suffered from a severe surgical operation, and it was believed by his friends impossible that he could survive the infliction of imprisonment. The Rev. John Browne writes: 'A committee very generously formed at Ipswich undertook the management of his affairs, and when they learned at the end of eleven days' imprisonment that he had undergone a most severe attack, indicating at least the possibility of sudden death, they sent a deputation to the Court to pay the sum demanded. The Court, however, required, as well as the money, the usual oath of canonical obedience, and this Mr. Childs refused to give. He was told by p. 148his friends that he would surely die in prison, but his reply was, 'That is not my business.' But it seems so much had been made of the matter by the newspapers that Mr. Childs was released without taking the oath. Charles Childs, the son, followed in his father's steps. At Bungay the Churchmen seemed to have determined to make Dissenters as uncomfortable as possible. Actually five years after they had thrown the father into prison, the churchwardens proceeded against the son, having been baffled in repeated attempts to distrain upon his goods, and cited him into the Ecclesiastical Court, where it took two and a half years to determine whether the sum of three shillings and fourpence was due. At the end of that time the judge decided it was not, and the churchwardens had to pay Mr. Childs' costs as well as their own, which in the course of time amounted to a very respectable sum. Charles Childs, who died suddenly a few years since, and who never seemed to me to have aged a day since I first knew him, was truly a chip of the old block. He was much in London, as he printed quite as much as his father for the leading London publishers. An enlightened patriot, he was in very many cases successful in resisting the obstacles p. 149raised from time to time by party spirit or Church bigotry. On more than one occasion he conducted a number of his workmen through an illegally-closed path, and opened it by the destruction of the fences, repeated appeals to the persistent obstructions having proved unavailing. He was a man of scholarly and literary attainments, a clever talker, well able to hold his own, and during the Corn Law and Currency agitation he contributed one or more articles on these subjects to the *Westminster Review*, then edited by his friend, the late General Perronet Thompson, a very foremost figure in Radical circles forty years ago, always trying to get into Parliament—rarely succeeding in the attempt. 'How can he expect it,' said Mr. Cobden to me one day, 'when, instead of going to the principal people to support him, he finds out some small tradesman—some little tailor or shoemaker—to introduce him?' Once upon a time the *Times* furiously attacked Charles Childs. His reply, which was able and convincing, was forwarded, but only procured admission in the shape of an advertisement, for which Mr. Childs had to pay ten pounds. The corner of East Anglia of which I write rarely produced two better men than the Childs, father and son. They are gone, p. 150but the printing business still survives, though no longer carried on under the well-known name. By their noble integrity and public spirit they proved themselves worthy of a craft to which light and literature and leading owe so much. It is to such men that England is under lasting obligations, and one of the indirect benefits of a State Church is that it gives them a grievance, and a sense of wrong, which compels them to gird up their energies to act the part of village Hampdens or guiltless Cromwells. All the manhood in them is aroused and strengthened as they contend for what they deem right and just, and against force and falsehood. Poets, we are told, by one himself a poet,

> 'Are cradled into poetry by wrong;
> They learn in suffering what they teach in song.'

Nonconformists have cause especially to rejoice in the bigotry and persecution to which they have been exposed, since it has led them by a way they knew not, to become the champions of a broader creed and a more general right than that of which their fathers dreamed. It is easy to swim with the stream; it requires a strong man to swim against it. Two hundred years of such swimming had made the Bungay Nonconformists strong, and p. 151gave to the world two such exceptionally sturdy and strengthful men as John and Charles Childs. I was proud to know them as a boy; in advancing years I am prouder still to be permitted to bear this humble testimony to their honest worth. It is because Nonconformity has raised up such men in all parts of the land, that a higher tone has been given to our public life, that politics mean something more than a struggle between the ins and the outs, and that 'Onward' is our battle-cry.

Of the young men more or less coming under the influence of the Childs's, perhaps one of the most successful was the late Bernard Bolingbroke Woodward, Librarian to her Majesty. When I first knew him he was in a bank at Norwich. Thence he passed to Highbury College, and in due time, after he had taken his B.A. degree, settled as the Independent minister at Wortwell, near Harleston, in Norfolk. There he became connected with John Childs, and, amidst much hard work, edited for the firm a new edition of 'Barclay's Universal English Dictionary.' In 1860, on the death of Mr. Glover, who had for many years filled the post of Librarian to the Queen at Windsor Castle, Mr. Woodward's name p. 152was mentioned to the Prince, in reply to inquiries for a competent successor. Acting on the advice of a friend at head-quarters, Mr. Woodward forwarded to Prince Albert the same printed testimonials which he had sent in when he was a candidate for the vacant secretaryship of a large and popular society, and to those alone he owed his appointment to the office of Librarian to the Queen. An interview took place at Windsor Castle, which was highly satisfactory; but before the appointment was finally made, Mr. Woodward informed Her Majesty and the Prince that there was one circumstance which he had omitted to mention, and which might disqualify him for the post. 'Pray, what is that disqualification?' asked the Prince. 'It is,' replied Mr. Woodward, 'that I have been educated for, and have actually conducted the services of an Independent congregation in the country.' 'And why should that be thought to disqualify you?' asked the Prince. 'It does nothing of the sort. If that is all, we are quite satisfied, and feel perfectly safe in having you for a librarian.' Am I not justified in saying that at one time Bungay influences reached far and near?

p. 153CHAPTER VI.
a celebrated norfolk town.

Great Yarmouth Nonconformists — Intellectual life — Dawson Turner — Astley Cooper — Hudson Gurney — Mrs. Bendish.

When David Copperfield, Dickens tells us, first caught sight of Yarmouth, it seemed to him to look rather spongy and soppy. As he drew nearer, he remarks, 'and saw the whole adjacent prospect, lying like a straight, low line under the sky, I hinted to Peggotty that a mound or so might have improved it, and also that if the land had been a little more separated from the sea, and the town and the tide had not been quite so much mixed up, like toast-and-water, it would have been much nicer.' He adds: 'When we got into the street, which was strange to me, and smelt the fish, and pitch, and oakum, and tallow, and saw the sailors walking about, and the carts jingling up and down over the stones, I felt that I had done so busy a place injustice.' In this opinion his readers who know p. 154Yarmouth will agree. Brighton and Hastings and Eastbourne might envy Yarmouth its sandy beach, where you can lead an amphibious life, watching the fishing-smacks as they come to shore with cargoes often so heavy as to be sold for manure; watching the merchant-ships and yachts that lie securely in the Roads, or the long trail of black smoke of Scotch or northern steamers far away; watching the gulls ever skimming the surface of the waves; or the children, as they build little forts and dwellings in the sand to be rudely swept to destruction by the advancing tide. In the golden light of summer, how blue is the sky, how green the sea, how yellow the sand, how jolly look the men and handsome the women! What health and healing are in the air, as it comes laden with ozone from the North Sea! You have the sea in front and on each side to look at, to walk by, to splash in, to sail on. The danger is, that you grow too fat, too ruddy, too hearty, too boisterous. As we all know, Venus was born out of the sea, and out there on that eastern peninsula, of which Yarmouth is the pride and ornament, there used to flourish bonny lasses, as if to show that the connection between the ocean and lovely woman is as intimate as of yore. Yarmouth and Lowestoft owe a great p. 155deal to the Great Eastern Railway, which has made them places of health-resort from all parts of England; and truly the pleasure-seeker or the holiday-maker may go farther and fare worse.

I was a proud boy when first I set foot in Yarmouth. How I came to go there I can scarcely remember, but it is to be presumed I accompanied my father on one of those grand occasions—as far as Nonconformist circles are concerned—when the brethren met together for godly comfort and counsel. It is true Wrentham was in Suffolk, and Yarmouth was in Norfolk, but the Congregational Churches of that quarter had always been connected by Christian fellowship and sympathy, and hence I was taken to Yarmouth—at that time far more like a Dutch than an English town—and wonderful to me was the Quay, with its fine houses on one side and its long line of ships on the other—something like the far-famed Bompjes of Rotterdam—and the narrow rows in which the majority of the labouring classes were accustomed to live. 'A row,' wrote Charles Dickens, 'is a long, narrow lane or alley, quite straight, or as nearly so as may be, with houses on each side, both of which you can sometimes touch with the finger-tips of each hand by stretching out your arms to their full extent. p. 156Many and many a picturesque old bit of domestic architecture is to be hunted up among the rows. In some there is little more than a blank wall for the double boundary. In others the houses retreat into busy square courts, where washing and clear-starching are done, and wonderful nasturtiums and scarlet-runners are reared from green boxes filled with that scarce commodity, vegetable mould. Most of these rows are paved with pebbles from the beach, and to traverse them a peculiar form of low cart, drawn by a single horse, is employed.' This to me was a great novelty, as with waggons and carts I was familiar, but not with a Yarmouth cart—now, I find, replaced by wheelbarrows. In Amsterdam, at the present day, you may see many such quaint old rows. But in Amsterdam you have an evil-smelling air, while in Yarmouth it is ever fresh and crisp, and redolent, as it were, of the neighbouring sea. The market-place and the big church were at the back of this congeries of quays and rows, and the sea and the old pier were at quite a respectable distance from the town. I fancy the Yarmouth of the London bathers has now extended down to the sandy beach, and the rough and rude old pier has given place to one better adapted to the wants and requirements of an p. 157increasingly well-to-do community. Far more Dutch than English was the Yarmouth of half a century ago, I again say.

As to the Yarmouth Independent parson, I shall never forget him. He was a very big man, with great red cheeks that hung over his collar like blown bladders, and was always on stilts. He preached in a big meeting-house, now no more, the pillars of which intercepted alike the view and the sound. One winter evening he was holding forth, in his usual heavy style, to a few good people—with whom, evidently, all pleasure was out of the question—who came there, as in duty bound, and sat like martyrs all the while, and all were as grave as the preacher, when a wicked boy rushed in and, in a hurried manner, called out, 'Fire! fire!' The effect, I am told, was electrical. For once the good parson was in a hurry, and moved as quickly and spoke as rapidly as his fellows; but never had there been so much excitement in his chapel since he had been its pastor. Once, I remember, he came to town, and dropped in at the close of a party rather convivially inclined, in the Old London Coffee House. As the reverend gentleman advanced to greet his friends, a London lawyer, with all the impudence of his class, muttered, p. 158in a whisper intended to be heard, and which was heard, by everyone, 'Yarmouth bloater.' The good man said nothing, but it was evident he thought all the more, as the group were more or less tittering over the fitness of the comparison. The lawyer who made the remark was also the son of a London minister, and, therefore, might have been expected to have known better. I fear the Yarmouth minister never forgave him. Well, it only served him right, as he had a horrible way of making young people very uncomfortable. 'Well, Master James,' said he to me on one occasion, when all the brethren had come to dine at Wrentham, and when I was admitted, in conformity with the golden maxim in all well-regulated family circles, that little children were to be seen and not heard (perhaps in our day the fault is too much in an opposite direction), 'can you inform me which is the more proper form of expression—a pair of new gloves, or a new pair of gloves?' Of course I gave the wrong answer, as I blushed up to the ears at finding myself the smallest personage in the room, publicly appealed to by the biggest. He meant well, I dare say. His only object was to draw me out; but the question and the questioner gave me a bad quarter of an hour, and I never got p. 159over the unpleasant sensation of which he had unconsciously been the originator in my youthful breast.

At that time Yarmouth people were supposed to be a little superior. They were well-to-do, and lived in good style, and, as was to be expected, considering the sanitary advantages of the situation, were in good health and spirits. They got a good deal of their intellectual character from Norwich, which at the time set the fashion in such matters. In 1790 two societies were established in that city for the private and amicable discussion of miscellaneous questions. One of these, the Tusculan, seems to have devoted the attention of its members exclusively to political topics; while the Speculative, although it imposed no restrictions on the range of inquiry, was of a more philosophical character. William Taylor was a member of both, and it is difficult to say whether he distinguished himself most by his ingenuity in debate, by the novelty of the information which he brought to bear on every point, or by the lively sallies of imagination with which he at once amused and excited his hearers. The papers read by himself embraced an infinite variety of subjects, from the theory of the earth, then unillumined by p. 160the disclosures of modern geologists, to the most elaborate and refined productions of its rational tenants, and he was seldom at a loss to place on new ground or in a fresh light the matter of discussion introduced by others. Writers of every tongue, studied by him with observant curiosity, stored his retentive memory with materials ready to be applied on every occasion, moulded by his Promethean talent into the most animated and alluring forms. As a speaker and converser he was eminently characterized by a constant flow of brilliant ideas, by a rapid succession of striking images, and by a never-failing copiousness of words, often quaint, but always correct. A similar society was formed at Yarmouth, under the auspices of Dr. Aiken, at which William Taylor also occasionally attended. The Rev. Thomas Compton has given the following description of these visits: 'We were, moreover, sometimes gratified by the presence of our literary friends from Norwich. I have there repeatedly listened to the mild and persuasive eloquence of the late Dr. Enfield. A gentleman, too, still living, who has lately added to his literary fame by a biographical work of high repute (I scarcely need add that I allude to Mr. W. Taylor) would sometimes instruct us by his p. 161various and profound knowledge, or amuse us with his ingenious paradoxes.' When we recollect how at this time the poetical puerilities of Bath Easton flourished in the West, we may claim that Norwich and Yarmouth, if not as favoured by fashion, had at any rate a claim to intellectual reputation at least quite equal to that city of the *ton*. Dr. Sayers, whose biography William Taylor had written, and whose 'Dramatic Sketches of Northern Mythology' had created a great sensation at the time, was of Yarmouth extraction.

The Rev. Mr. Compton writes: 'In Yarmouth, where I lived at this time, and where Lord Chedworth was accustomed to pay an annual visit, there was then a society of gentlemen who met once a fortnight for the purpose of amicable discussion. Our members—alas! how few remain—were of all parties and persuasions, and some of them of very distinguished attainments. A society thus constituted was in those days as pleasant as it was instructive. The most eager disputation was never found to endanger the most perfect goodwill, nor did any bitter feuds arise from this entire freedom of opinion till the prolific period of the French Revolution. On this subject our controversies became very impassioned. The present Sir Astley p. 162Cooper, then a very young man, was accustomed to pass his vacations with his most excellent father, Dr. Cooper, a name ever to be by me beloved and revered. It was the amusement of our young friend to say things of the most irritating nature, I believe—like Lady Florence Pemberton in the novel—merely to see who would make the ugliest face. Thus circumstanced, it was not in my philosophy to be the coolest of the party.' We can well imagine the consequences. There was a row, and the literary society came to grief. As time went on matters became worse instead of better, and the town was split up into parties—Liberal or the reverse, Church or Dissent, but all of one mind as regards their views being correct; and as to the weakness or wickedness of persons who thought otherwise. The evil of this spirit knew no bounds, and the demoralizing effect it produced was especially apparent at election times. When Oldfield wrote his 'Origin of Parliaments,' the town, he tells us, was under the influence of the Earl of Leicester, and was for many years represented by some of his Lordship's family. The right of election was in the burgesses at large, of whom there were at that time one thousand. The Reform Bill did little to improve the state of p. 163affairs; it led to greater bribery and corruption and intimidation than ever, and now, as a Parliamentary borough, Yarmouth has ceased to exist. 'Sugar,' it seems, was the slang term used for money, and the honest voters were too eager to get it. Alas! in none of our seaport towns is the standard of morality very high. Yarmouth, at any rate, is not worse than Deal. In old days the excitement of a Yarmouth election much affected our village. It lasted some days. The outvoters were brought from the uttermost parts of the earth. As there were no railways, stage-coaches were hired to bring them down from town; and when they changed horses at Wrentham, quite a crowd would assemble to look at the flags, and the free and independents on their way to do their duty, overflowing with enthusiasm and beer.

Sir Astley Cooper was much connected with Yarmouth in his young days, when his father was the incumbent of the parish church. Some of his boyish pranks were peculiar. Here is one of them: 'Having taken two pillows from his mother's bed, he carried them up the spire of Yarmouth Church, at a time when the wind was blowing from the north-east; and as soon as he p. 164had ascended as high as he could, he ripped them open, and, shaking out their contents, dispersed them in the air. The feathers were carried away by the wind, and fell far and wide over the surface of the market-place, to the great astonishment of a large number of persons assembled there. The timid looked upon it phenomenon predictive of some calamity; the inquisitive formed a thousand conjectures; while some, curious in natural history, actually accounted for it by a gale of wind in the north blowing wild-fowl feathers from the island of St. Paul's.' On another occasion he got into an old trunk, which the family had agreed to get rid of as inconvenient in the house. In this case he had to pay the penalty, when he emerged from the chest in the carpenter's shop. The men, who had complained terribly of its weight, were not inclined to allow young Astley to get off free. One of Astley's tricks had, however, a good motive, as it was intended to cure an old woman of her besetting sin—a tendency to take a drop too much. In order to cure the old woman of this weakness, he dressed himself as well as he could to represent the sable form of his satanic majesty. Alas! instead of being surprised, the old lady was too far-gone for that, and listened with tipsy gravity to the p. 165distinguished visitor's discourse. In her case it was true, as Burns wrote:

'Wi' tipenny we fear nae evil;
Wi' usquebae we'll face the deevil.'

One of his tricks nearly led to unpleasant consequences. Whilst out shooting one day, near Yarmouth, he killed an owl—a bird familiarly known in Yarmouth by the sobriquet of 'Brother Billy.' Having arrived at home, he went up into his mother's room, with the bird concealed behind his coat, and, assuming a countenance full of fear and sorrow, exclaimed, 'Mother, mother, I've shot my brother Billy!' but the alarm and distress instantly depicted on the distracted countenance of his parent induced him as quickly as possible to pull the owl from under his coat. This at once exposed the truth and allayed the apprehensions of his mother's mind, but the effects of the shock it caused did not so immediately pass away. Dr. Cooper determined to punish his son, and he therefore confined him, according to his usual mode of correction, in his own house. Astley was, however, but little disposed to remain passive in his imprisonment, and in the wantonness of his ever-active disposition amused himself by climbing up the chimney, and having at length reached the p. 166summit, endeavoured, by imitating the well-known tone of the chimney-sweeper, and calling out as lustily as he could, 'Sweep, sweep!' to attract the attention of the people below. Even on his father the incorrigible lad seems on more than one occasion to have tried his little game. One day, while the worthy Doctor was marrying a couple in the church, Master Astley concealed himself in a turret close by the altar, and, imitating his father's voice, repeated in a subdued tone the words of the marriage-service as the ceremony proceeded, to the consternation of his father, who said that he had never observed an echo in that place before. Once or twice the lad's life was in peril, as when his foot slipped on the top of the church, and he was unpleasantly suspended for some time between the rafters of the ceiling and the floor of the chancel. On another occasion he had a narrow escape from drowning. It seems that on the Yare are little boats out together very slightly, for the purpose of carrying a man, his gun, and dog over the shallows of Braydon, in pursuit of the flights of wild-fowl which at certain seasons haunt these shoals. When the boat is thus loaded, it only draws two or three inches of water, and is quite unfit for sea. Young Astley nearly lost his life p. 167in attempting to take one of these boats out to open sea. In this way young Astley Cooper, from his fearless and enterprising disposition, soon became a sort of leader of the Yarmouth boys, and at their head, for a time, seems to have devoted himself to every kind of amusement within his reach — riding, boating, fishing, and not unfrequently sports of a less harmless character, such as breaking lamps and windows, ringing the church bells at all hours, disturbing the people by frequent alterations of the church clock, so that if any mischief were committed it was sure, says his admiring biographer, to be set down to him.

The two men who shed most literary fame on the Yarmouth of my childhood were Dawson Turner and Hudson Gurney, who in this respect resembled each other, that they were both bankers and both antiquarians more or less distinguished. Dawson Turner was a man of middle height and of saturnine aspect, who had the reputation of being a hard taskmaster to the ladies of his family, who were quite as intelligent and devoted to literature as himself. He published a 'Tour in Normandy' — at that time scarcely anyone travelled abroad — and much other matter, and perhaps as an autograph-collector was unrivalled. Most of p. 168his books, with his notes, more or less valuable, are now in the British Museum. Sir Charles Lyell, when a young man, visited the Turner family in 1817, and gives us a very high idea of them all. 'Mr. Turner,' he says, in a letter to his father, 'surprises me as much as ever. He wrote twenty-two letters last night after he had wished us "Good-night." It kept him up till two o'clock this morning.' Again Sir Charles writes: 'What I see going on every hour in this family makes me ashamed of the most active day I ever spent at Midhurst. Mrs. Turner has been etching with her daughters in the parlour every morning at half-past six.' Of Hudson Gurney in his youth we get a flattering portrait in one of the charming 'Remains of the Late Mrs. Trench,' edited by her son, Archbishop of Dublin. Writing from Yarmouth in 1799, she says: 'I have been detained here since last Friday, waiting for a fair wind, and my imprisonment would have been comfortless enough had it not have been for the attention of Mr. Hudson Gurney, a young man on whom I had no claims except from a letter of

Mr. Sanford's, who, without knowing him, or having any connection with him, recommended me to his care, feeling wretched that I should be unprotected in the first p. 169part of my journey. He has already devoted to me one evening and two mornings, assisted me in money matters, lent me books, and enlivened my confinement to a wretched room by his pleasant conversation. Mr. Sanford having described me as a person travelling about *for her health*, he says his old assistant in the Bank fancied I was a decrepit elderly lady who might safely be consigned to his youthful partner. His description of his surprise thus prepared was conceived in a very good strain of flattery. He is almost two-and-twenty, understands several languages, seems to delight in books, and to be uncommonly well informed.' Little credit, however, is due to Mr. Hudson Gurney for his politeness in this case. The lovely and lively widow—she had married Colonel St. George at the age of eighteen, and the marriage only lasted two or three years, the Colonel dying of consumption—must have possessed personal and mental attractions irresistible to a cultivated young man of twenty-two. Had she been old and ugly, it is to be feared his business engagements would have prevented the youthful banker devoting much time to her ladyship's service.

Yarmouth is intimately connected with literature and the fine arts. It was off Yarmouth that p. 170Robinson Crusoe was shipwrecked; and the testimony he bears to the character of the people shows how kindly disposed were the Yarmouth people of his day. 'We,' he writes, 'got all safe on shore, and walked afterwards on foot to Yarmouth, where, as unfortunate men, we were used with great humanity, not only by the magistrates of the town, who assigned us good quarters, but also by particular merchants and owners of ships, and had money given us, sufficient to carry us either to London or back to Hull, as we thought fit.' It was from Yarmouth that Wordsworth and Coleridge sailed away to Germany, then almost a *terra incognita*. Leman Blanchard was born at Yarmouth, as well as Sayers, the first, if not the cleverest, of our English caricaturists. One of the most brilliant men ever returned to Parliament was Winthrop Mackworth Praed, M.P. for Yarmouth, whose politics as a boy I detested as much as in after-years I learned to admire his genius. One of the most fortunate men of our day, Sir James Paget, the great surgeon, was a Yarmouth lad, and the See of Chester was filled by an accomplished divine, also a Yarmouth lad. Southey, when at Yarmouth, where his brother was a student for some time, was so much struck with p. 171the uniqueness of the epitaphs in the Yarmouth Church, that he took the trouble to copy many of them. One was as follows:

> 'We put him out to nurse;
> Alas! his life he paid,
> But judge not; he was overlaid.'

And hence it may be inferred that in Yarmouth the custom of baby-farming has long flourished. Possibly thence it may have extended itself to London. Amongst the truly great men who have lived and died in Yarmouth, honourable mention must be made of Hales, the Norfolk Giant. In times past soldiers and sailors and royal personages were often to be seen at Yarmouth. It was at Yarmouth the heroes, returning from many a distant battle-field, often landed. Nelson on one occasion—that is, after the affair of Copenhagen—when he landed, at once made his way to the hospital to see his men. To one of them, who had lost his arm, he said, 'There, Jack, you and I are spoiled for fishermen.'

A good deal of Puritanism seems to have come into England by way of Yarmouth. In Queen Elizabeth's time, 300 Flemings settled there, who had fled from Popery and Spain in their native land. In Norwich the Dutch Church p. 172remains to this day. Some of them seem to have been the friends and teachers of the far-famed, and I believe unjustly maligned, Robert Browne. In Norfolk the seed fell upon good soil. While sacerdotalism was more or less being developed in the State Church, the Norfolk men boldly protested against Papal abominations, as they deemed them, and swore to maintain the gospel of Geneva and Knox. One of the men imprisoned when Bancroft was Archbishop of Canterbury, for attending a conventicle, was Thomas Ladd, 'a merchant of Yarmouth.' The writ ran: 'Because that, on the Sabbath days, after the sermons ended, sojourning in the house of Mr. Jachler, in Yarmouth, who was late preacher in Yarmouth, joined with him in repeating the substance and heads of the sermons that day made in the church, at which Thomas Ladd was usually present.' In 1624 the penal laws for suppressing Separatists were strictly enforced in Yarmouth, and one of the teachers of a small society of Anabaptists was cast into prison, and the Bishop of Norwich wrote a letter of thanks to the bailiffs for their activity in this matter, which is preserved to this day. But, nevertheless, people still continued to worship God according to the p. 173dictates of conscience; we find the Earl of Dorset in his reply to the town of Yarmouth, as to the way in which the town should be governed, adds: 'I should want in my care of you if I should not let you know that his Majesty is not only informed, but incensed against you for conniving at and tolerating a company of Brownists among you. I pray you remember there was no seam in the Saviour's garment.' Bridge was the founder of the Yarmouth Congregational Church, somewhere about the time of the commencement of the Civil War. The people declared for the Parliament. Colonel Goffe was one of its representatives in the House of Commons. All along, the town seems to have been puritanically inclined, and to have been in this matter more independent than neighbouring towns. At one time they were so tolerant that the Independents seem to have worshipped in one end of the church while the regular clergyman performed the service in the other; but that did not last long, and when the Independents had a place of worship of their own, they were not a little troubled by Friends and Papists claiming for themselves the liberty the Independents had sought and won. In 1655 the peace of the Church was disturbed by Quaker doctrines. It appears two females, members p. 174of the Church, had joined them, and refused to return. We read: 'The messenger appointed to visit May Rouse, brought in an account of her disowning and despising the Church; she would not come at all unless she had a message from the Spirit moving her.' She came, however, a week after (December 11), but by reason of the cold weather was desired to come in again the next Tuesday. She did so, and gave in these two reasons why she forsook the Church: 1. Because the doctrine of the Gospel of Faith was not holden forth; 2. Because there wanted the right administration of baptism.

In 1659 the Church at Yarmouth, feeling the times to be full of trouble and of peril, said:

'1. We judge a Parliament to be expedient for the preservation of the peace of these nations; and withal, we do desire that all due care be taken that the Parliament be such as may preserve the interests of Christ and His people in these nations.

'2. As touching the magistrates' power in matters of faith and worship, we have declared our judgments in our late (Free Savoy) confession, and though we greatly prize our Christian liberties, yet we profess our utter dislike and abhorrence of p. 175a universal toleration, as being contrary to the mind of God in His Word.

'3. We judge that the taking away of tithes for the maintenance of ministers until as full a maintenance be equally secured and as legally settled, tends very much to the destruction of the ministry, and the preaching of the Gospel in these nations.

'4. It is our desire that countenance be not given unto, nor trust reposed in, the hand of Quakers, they being persons of such principles as are destructive to the Gospel, and inconsistent with the peace of modern societies.'

In five years the Yarmouth people had a Roland for their Oliver; the King had got his own again, and he and the Parliament of the day looked upon the Independents or Presbyterians as mischievous as the Quakers; and as to tithes, they were quite as much resolved, the only difference being that King and Parliament insisted on their being paid to Episcopalians alone. In 1770 Lady Huntingdon writes: 'Success has crowned our labours in that wicked place, Yarmouth.'

Mrs. Bendish, in whom the Protector was said to have lived again, was quite a character in Yarmouth society. Bridget Ireton, the granddaughter p. 176of the Protector, married in 1669 Mr. Thomas Bendish, a descendant of Sir Thomas Bendish, baronet, Ambassador from Charles I. to the Sultan. She died in 1728, removing, however, in the latter years of her life to Yarmouth. Her name stands among the members of the church in London of which Caryl had been pastor, and over which Dr. Watts presided. To her the latter addressed at any rate one copy of verses to be found in his collected works. She recollected her grandfather, and standing, when six years old, between his knees at a State Council, she heard secrets which neither bribes nor whippings could extract from her. Her grandfather she held to be a saint in heaven, and only second to the Twelve Apostles. Asked one day whether she had ever been at Court, her reply was, 'I have never been at Court since I was waited upon on the knee.' Yet she managed to dispense with a good deal of waiting, and never would suffer a servant to attend her. God, she said, was a sufficient guard, and she would have no other. She is described as loquacious and eloquent and enthusiastic, frequenting the drawing-rooms and assemblies of Yarmouth, dressed in the richest silks, and with a small black hood on her head. When she left, which would be at one in the p. 177morning, perched on her old-fashioned saddle, she would trot home, piercing the night air with her loud, jubilant psalms, in which she described herself as one of the elect, in a tone more remarkable for strength than sweetness. In the daytime she would work with her labourers, taking her turn at the pitchfork or the spade. The old Court dresses of her mother and Mrs. Cromwell were bequeathed by her to Mrs. Robert Luson, of Yarmouth, and were shown as recently as 1834, at an exhibition of Court dresses held at the Somerset Gallery in the Strand. As was to be expected, Mrs. Bendish was enthusiastic in the cause of the Revolution of 1688, and the printed sheets relating to it were dropped by her secretly in the streets of Yarmouth, to prepare the people for the good time coming. Her son was a friend of Dr. Watts as well as his mother. He died at Yarmouth, unmarried, in the year 1753, and with him the line of Bendish seems to have come to an end. Another daughter of Ireton was married to Nathaniel Carter, who died in 1723, aged 78. His father, John Carter, was commander-in-chief of the militia of the town in 1654. He subscribed the Solemn League and Covenant, being then one of the elders of the Independent congregation. He was also bailiff of p. 178the town, and an intimate friend of Ireton. He died in 1667. On his tombstone we read:

> 'His course, his fight, his race,
> Thus finished, fought, and run,
> Death brings him to the place
> From whence is no return.'

He lived at No. 4, South Quay, and it was there, so it is said, that the resolve was made that King Charles should die.

He is gone, but his room still remains unaltered—a large wainscoted upper chamber, thirty feet long, with three windows looking on to the quay, with carved and ornamented chimney-piece and ceiling. A great obscurity, as was to be expected, hangs over the transaction, as even now there are men who shrink from lifting up a finger against the Lord's anointed. Dinner had been ordered at four, but it was not till eleven, that it was served, and that the die had been cast. The members of the Secret Council, we are told, 'after a very short repast, immediately set off by post—many for London, and some for the quarters of the army.' Such is the account given in a letter, written in 1773, by Mr. Mewling Luson, a well-known resident in Yarmouth, whose father, Mr. William Luson, was nearly connected the p. 179Cromwell family. Nathaniel Carter, the son-in-law of Ireton, was in the habit of showing the room, and relating the occurrence connected with it, which happened when he was a boy. Cromwell was not at that council. He never was in Yarmouth; but that there was such consultation there is more than probable. Yarmouth was full of Cromwellites. In the Market Place, now known as the Weavers' Arms, to this day is shown the panelled parlour whence Miles Corbet was used to go forth to worship in that part of the church allotted to the Independents. Miles Corbet was the son of Sir Thomas Corbet, of Sprouston, who had been made Recorder of Yarmouth in the first year of Charles, and who was one of the representatives of the town in the Long Parliament. The son was an ardent supporter of the policy of Cromwell, and, like him, laboured that England might be religious and free and great, as she never could be under any king of the Stuart race; and he met with his reward. 'See, young man,' said an old man to Wilberforce, as he pointed to a figure of Christ on the cross, 'see the fate of a Reformer.' It was so emphatically with Miles Corbet. Under the date of 1662 there is the following entry in the church-book:

p. 180'1662.—Miles Corbet suffered in London.'

He was a member of the church there, and was one of the judges who sat on the trial of King Charles I. His name stands last on the list of those who signed the warrant for that monarch's execution. Corbet fled into Holland at the Restoration, with Colonels Okey and Barkstead. George Downing—a name ever infamous—had been Colonel Okey's chaplain. He became a Royalist at the Restoration, and was despatched as Envoy Extraordinary into Holland, where, under a promise of safety, he trepanned the three persons above named into his power, and sent them over to England to suffer death for having been members of the Commission for trying King

Charles I. For this service he was created a baronet. The King sent an order to the Sheriffs of London on April 21, 1662, that Okey's head and quarters should have Christian burial, as he had manifested some signs of contrition; but Barkstead's head was directed to be placed on the Traitor's Gate in the Tower, and Corbet's head on the bridge, and their quarters on the City gates.

Foremost amongst the noted women of the Independent Church must be mentioned Sarah Martin, of whose life a sketch appeared in the p. 181 *Edinburgh Review* as far back as 1847. A life of her was also published by the Religious Tract Society. Sarah, who joined the Yarmouth church in 1811, was born at Caistor. From her nineteenth year she devoted her only day of rest, the Sabbath, to the task of teaching in a Sunday-school. She likewise visited the inmates of the workhouse, and read the Scriptures to the aged and the sick. But the gaol was the scene of her greatest labours. In 1819, after some difficulty, she obtained admission to it, and soon seems to have acquired an extraordinary influence over the minds of the prisoners. She then gave up one day in the week to instruct them in reading and writing. At length she attended the prison regularly, and kept an exact account of her proceedings and their results in a book, which is now preserved in the public library of the town. As there was no chaplain, she read and preached to the inmates herself, and devised means of obtaining employment for them. She continued this good work till the end of her days in 1843, when she died, aged fifty-three. A handsome window of stained glass, costing upwards of #100, raised by subscription, has been placed to her memory in the west window of the north aisle of St. Nicholas Church. But p. 182her fame extends beyond local limits, and is part of the inheritance of the universal Church. It was in Mr. Walford's time that Sarah Martin commenced her work. Mr. Walford tells us, in his Autobiography, that the Church had somewhat degenerated in his day, that the line of thought was worldly, and not such as became the Gospel. It is clear that in his time it greatly revived, and, even as a lad, the intelligence of the congregation seemed to lift me up into quite a new sphere, so different were the merchants and ship-owners of Yarmouth from the rustic inhabitants of my native village. In this respect, if I remember aright, the family of Shelley were particularly distinguished. One dear old lady, who lived at the

Quay, was emphatically the minister's friend. She had a nice house of her own and ample means, and there she welcomed ministers and their wives and children. It is to be hoped, for the sake of poor parsons, that such people still live. I know it was a great treat to me to enjoy the hospitality of the kind-hearted Mrs. Goderham, for whose memory I still cherish an affectionate regard. To live in one of the best houses on the Quay, and to lie in my bed and to see through the windows the masts of the shipping, was indeed to a boy a treat.

p. 183A little while ago I chanced to be at Norwich, when the thought naturally occurred to me that I would take a run to Yarmouth—a journey quickly made by the rail. In my case the journey was safely and expeditiously accomplished, and I hastened once more to revisit the scenes and associations of my youth. Alas! wherever I went I found changes. A new generation had arisen that knew not Joseph. The wind was howling down the Quay; the sand was blown into my mouth, my nose, my ears; I could scarcely see for the latter, or walk for the former; but, nevertheless, I made my way to the pier. Only one person was on it, and his back was turned to me. As he stood at the extreme end, with chest expanded, with mouth wide open, as if prepared to swallow the raging sea in front and the Dutch coast farther off, I thought I knew the figure. It was a reporter from Fleet Street and he was the only man to greet me in the town I once knew so well. Yes; the Yarmouth of my youth was gone. Then a reporter from Fleet Street was an individual never dreamt of. And so the world changes, and we get new men, fresh faces, other minds. The antiquarian Camden, were he to revisit Yarmouth, would not be a little astonished at what he would see. He wrote: 'As p. 184soon as the Yare has passed Claxton, it takes a turn to the south, that it may descend more gently into the sea, by which means it makes a sort of little tongue or slip of land, washt on one side by itself, on the other side by the sea. In this slip, upon an open shore, I saw Yarmouth, a very neat harbour and town, fortified both by the nature of the place and the contrivance of art. For, though it be almost surrounded with water, on the west with a river, over which there is a drawbridge, and on either side with the sea, except to the north, where it is joined to the continent; yet it is fenced with strong, stately walls, which, with the river, figure it into an oblong quadrangle. Besides the towers upon these, there is a mole or mount, to the east, from whence the great guns command the sea (scarce half a mile distant) all round. It has but one church, though very large and with a stately high spire, built near the north gate by Herbert, Bishop of Norwich.' In only one respect the Yarmouth of to-day resembles that of Camden's time. Then the north wind played the tyrant and plagued the coast, and it does so still.

p. 185CHAPTER VII.
the norfolk capital.

Brigg's Lane—The carrier's cart—Reform demonstration—The old dragon—Chairing M.P.'s—Hornbutton Jack—Norwich artists and literati—Quakers and Nonconformists.

Many, many years ago, when wandering in the North of Germany, I came to an hotel in the Fremden Buch, of which (Englishmen at that time were far more patriotic and less cosmopolitan than in these degenerate days) an enthusiastic Englishman had written—and possibly the writing had been suggested by the hard fare and dirty ways of the place:

'England, with all thy faults, I love thee still.'

Underneath, a still more enthusiastic Englishman had written: 'Faults? What faults? I know of none, except that Brigg's Lane, Norwich, wants widening.' For the benefit of the reader who may be a stranger to the locality, let me inform him that p. 186Brigg's Lane leads out of the fine Market Place, for which the good old city of Norwich is celebrated all the world over, and that on a recent visit to Norwich I found that the one fault which could be laid at the door of England had been removed—that Brigg's Lane had been widened—that, in fact, it had ceased to be a lane, and had been elevated into the dignity of a street.

My first acquaintance with Norwich, when I was a lad of tender years and of limited experience, was by Brigg's Lane. I had reached it by means of a carrier's cart—the only mode of conveyance between Southwold, Wrentham, Beccles and Norwich—a carrier's cart with a hood drawn by three noble horses, and able to accommodate almost any number of travellers and any amount of luggage. As the driver was well known to everyone, there was also a good deal of conversation of a more or less friendly character. The cart took one day to reach Norwich—which was, and it may be is, the commercial emporium of all that district—and another day to return. The beauty of such a conveyance, as compared with the railway travelling of to-day, was that there was no occasion to be in a flurry if you wanted to travel by it. Goldsmith—for such was the proprietor and driver's name—when he came to p. 187a place was in no hurry to leave it. All the tradesmen in the village had hampers or boxes to return, and it took some time to collect them; or messages and notes to send, and it took some time to write them; and at the alehouse there was always a little gossip to be done while the horses enjoyed their pail of water or mouthful of hay. Even at the worst there was no fear of being left behind, as by dint of running and holloaing you might get up with the cart, unless you were very much behind indeed. But you may be sure that when the day came that I was to visit the great city of Norwich I was ready for the carrier's cart long before the carrier's cart was ready for me. Why was it, you ask, that the Norwich journey was undertaken? The answer is not difficult to give. The Reform agitation at that time had quickened the entire intellectual and social life of the people. At length had dawned the age of reason, and had come the rights of man. The victory had been won all along the line, and was to be celebrated in the most emphatic manner. We Dissenters rejoiced with exceeding joy; for we looked forward, as a natural result, to the restoration of that religious equality in the eye of the law of which we had been unrighteously deprived, p. 188and in consequence of which we had suffered in many ways. We joined, as a matter of course, in the celebration of the victory which we and the entire body of Reformers throughout the land had gained; and how could that be done better than by feeding the entire community on old English fare washed down by old English ale? And this was done as far as practicable everywhere. For instance, at Bungay there was a public feast in the Market Place, and on the town-pump the Messrs. Childs erected a printing-press, which they kept hard at work all day printing off papers intended to do honour to the great event their fellow-townsmen were celebrating in so jovial a manner. In Norwich the demonstration was to be of a more imposing character, and as an invitation had come to the heads of the family from an old friend, a minister out of work, and living more or less comfortably on his property, it seemed good to them to accept it, and to take me with them, deeming, possibly, that of two evils it was best to choose the least, and that I should be safer under their eye at Norwich than with no one to look after me at home. At any rate, be that as it may, the change was not a little welcome, and much did I see to wonder at in the old Castle, the new Gaol, the size p. 189of the city, the extent of the Market Place, the smartness of the people, and the glare of the shops. It well re-paid me for the ride of twenty-six miles and the jolting of the carri-er's cart along the dusty roads.

As I look into the mirror of the past, I see, alas! but a faded pic-ture of that wonderful banquet in Norwich to celebrate Reform. There was a procession with banners and music, which seemed to me endless, as it toiled along in the dust under the fierce sun of summer, the spectators cheering all the way. There were speeches, I dare say, though no word of them remains; but I have a distinct recollection of peeping into the tents or tent, where the diners were at work, and of receiving from some one or other of them a bit of plum-pudding prepared for that day, which seemed to me of unu-sual excellence. I have a distinct recollection also of the fireworks in the evening, the first I had ever seen, on the Castle plain, and of the dense crowd that had turned out to see the sight; but I can well remember that I enjoyed myself much, and that I was awfully tired when it was all over.

Another memory also comes to me in connection with the old Dragon,—not of Revelation, but of Norwich—a huge green mon-ster, which was usually p. 190kept in St. Andrew's Hall, and dragged out at the time of city festivities. Men inside of it carried it along the street, and the sight was terrible to see, as it had a fero-cious head and a villainous tail, and resembled nothing that is in the heaven above or the earth beneath or the waters under the earth. I fancy, however, since the schoolmaster has gone abroad, that kind of dragon has ceased to roar. I think it was at a Norwich election that I saw it for the first and the only time, and it followed in the procession formed to chair the Members—the Members being seat-ed in gorgeous array on chairs, borne on the heads of people, and every now and then, much to the delight of the mob, though I should imagine very little to his own, the chair, with the Member in it, was tossed up into the air, and by this means it was supposed the general public were able to get a view of their M.P. and to see what manner of man he was. It was in some such way that I, as a lad, realized, as I never else should have done, the red face and the pink-silk stockings of the Hon. Mr. Scarlett, the happy candidate who pretended to enjoy the fun, as with the best grace possible under the circumstances he smiled on the ladies in the windows of the street, as he was borne along and bowed to all. From p. 191my recollection of the chairing I saw that time, I am more inclined to admire the activity of Wilberforce, of whom we read, when elected for Hull, 'When the procession reached his mother's house, he sprang from the chair, and, presenting himself with surprising quickness at a projecting window—it was that of the nursery in which his child-hood had been passed—he addressed the populace with such complete effect that he was afterwards able to decide the election of its successor.' At Norwich the Hon. Mr. Scarlett did well in not attempting a similar display of agility. Perhaps, however, it is quite as well that we have got rid of the chairing and the humour—Heaven help us!—to which it gave rise on the part of an English mob.

There was a delightful flavour of antiquity about the Norwich of that day—its old fusty chapels and churches, its old bridges and narrow streets. All the people with whom I came into contact on that festival seemed to me well stricken in years. It was not so very long since, old Hornbutton Jack had been seen threading his way along its ancient streets. With a countenance much resembling the portraits of Erasmus, with gray hair hanging about his shoulders, with his hat drawn over his eyes and his hands behind him, as if in deep meditation; p. 192John Fransham, the Norwich metaphysician and mathematician, might well excite the curiosity of the casual observer, especially when I add that he was bandy-legged, that he was short of stature, that he wore a green jacket, a broad hat, large shoes, and short worsted stockings. A Norwich weaver had helped to make Fransham a philosopher. Wright said Fransham could discourse well on the nature and fitness of things. He possessed a purely philosophical spirit and a soul well purified from vulgar errors. Fransham made himself famous in his day. There is every reason to believe that he had been for some time tutor to Mr. Windham. He is once recorded to have spent a day with Dr. Parr. Many of his pupils became professional men; with one of them, Dr. Leeds, the reader of Foote's comedies, if such a one exists, may be acquainted. The tutor and his pupil, as Johnny Macpherson and Dr. Last, were actually exhibited on the stage. But to return to Norwich antiquities. I have a dim memory of some old place where the Dutch and Huguenot refugees were permitted to meet for worship, and even now I can recognise there the possibility of another Sir

Thomas Browne—unless the Norwich of my boyhood has undergone the destructive process we p. 193love to call improvement—not even disturbed in his quiet study by the storm of civil war, inditing his thoughts as follows: 'That crystal is nothing else but ice strongly congealed; that a diamond is softened or broken by the blood of a goat; that bays preserve from the mischief of lightning and thunder; that the horse hath no gall; that a kingfisher hanged by the bill showeth where the wind lay; that the flesh of peacocks corrupteth not;' and so on—questions, it may be, as pertinent as those learnedly discussed in half-crown magazines at the present day.

As a boy, I was chiefly familiar with Norwich crapes and bombazines and Norwich shawls, which at that time were making quite a sensation in the fashionable world. It was at a later time that I came to hear of Old Crome and the Norwich school. Of him writes Mr. Wedmore, that 'he died in a substantial square-built house, in what was a good street then, in the parish of St. George, Colegate, having begun as a workman, and ended as a bourgeois. He was a simple man, of genial company. To the end of his life he used to go of an evening to the public-house as to an informal club. In the privileged bar-parlour, behind the taps and glasses, he sat with his friends and the shopkeepers, p. 194talking of local things. But it is not to be supposed that because his life was from end to end a humble one, though prosperous even outwardly after its kind, Crome was deprived of the companionship most fitted to his genius, the stimulus that he most needed. The very existence of the Norwich Society of Artists settles that question. The local men hung on his words; he knew that he was not only making pictures, but a school. And in the quietness of a provincial city a coterie had been formed of men bent on the pursuit of an honest and homely art, and of these he was the chief.' Dying, his last words were, 'Hobbema, oh, Hobbema, how I loved thee!' In my young days Mr. John Sell Cotman chiefly represented Norwich, although in later times he became connected with King's College, London. A lady writes to me: 'I think it was in the summer of 1842 Mr. Cotman came down to Norwich to visit his son John, who at that time was occupying a house on St. Bennet's Road. He visited us at Thorpe several times, and was unusually well and in good spirits, with sketchbook or folio always in hand. His father and sisters, too, were then living in a small house at Thorpe, and from the balcony of their house, which looked over the valley of the Wensum, he made p. 195one of his last interesting sketches, twelve of which, after his death, the following year, were selected by his sons for publication.'

Evelyn gives us a pleasant picture of Norwich when he went there 'to see that famous scholar and physitian, Dr. T. Browne, author of the "Religio Medici" and "Vulgar Errors," etc., now lately knighted.' Evelyn continues: 'Next morning I went to see Sir Thomas Browne, with whom I had corresponded by letter, though I had never seen him before, his whole house and garden being a Paradise and cabinet of rarities, and that of the best collection, especially medals, books, plants and natural things. Amongst other curiosities, Sir Thomas has a collection of all the eggs of all the foule and birds he could procure; that country, especially the promonotary of Norfolck, being frequented, as he said, by severall kinds, which seldom or never go further into the land, as cranes, storkes, eagles, and a variety of water-foule. He led me to see all the remarkable places of this ancient citty, being one of the largest and certainly, after London, one of the noblest of England, for its venerable cathedrall, number of stately churches, cleannesse of the streetes and building of flints so exquisitely headed and squared, as I was much p. 196astonished at; but he told me they had lost the art of squaring the flints, in which at one time they so much excelled, and of which the churches, best houses, and walls are built.' Further, Evelyn tells us: 'The suburbs are large, the prospect sweete with other amenities, not omitting the flower-gardens, in which all the inhabitants excel. The fabric of stuffs brings a vast trade to this populous towne.'

Long has Norwich rejoiced in clever people. In the life of William Taylor, one of her most distinguished sons, we have a formidable array of illustrious Norwich personages, in whom, alas! at the present time the world takes no interest. Sir James Edward Smith, founder and first President of the Linnfan Society, ought not to be forgotten. Of Taylor himself Mackintosh wrote: 'I can still trace William Taylor by his Armenian dress, gliding through the crowd in Annual Reviews, Monthly Magazines, Athenfums, etc., rousing the stupid public by paradox, or correcting it by useful and seasonable truth. It is true that he does not speak the Armenian or any other tongue but the Taylorian, but I am so fond of his vigour and originality, that for his sake I have studied and learned the language. As the Hebrew is studied by one book, so is the Taylorian by me for another. p. 197He never deigns to write to me, but in print I doubt whether he has many readers who so much understand, relish, and tolerate him, for which he ought to reward me by some of his manuscript esoteries.' More may be said of William Taylor. It was he who made Walter Scott a poet. Taylor's spirited translation of Burger's 'Leonore' with the two well-known lines—

> 'Tramp, tramp along the land they rode,
> Splash, splash along the sea,'

opened up to Scott a field in which for a time he won fame and wealth.

Of Mrs. Taylor, wife of the grandson of the eminent Hebraist, Mackintosh declared that she was the Madame Roland of Norwich. We owe to her Mrs. Austen and Lady Duff Gordon. Mr. Reeve, the translator of De Tocqueville's 'Democracy,' has preserved the memory of his father, Dr. Henry Reeve, by the republication of his 'Journal of a Tour on the Continent.' Let me also mention that Dr. Caius, the founder of Caius College, Cambridge, was a Norwich man.

To Noncons Norwich offers peculiar attractions. We have in Dr. Williams's library 'The Order of the Prophesie in Norwich'; and Robinson, the leader of the Pilgrim Fathers, had a Norwich p. 198charge. Even in a later day some of the Norwich divines had a godly zeal for freedom, worthy of Milton himself, and on which the Pilgrim Fathers would have smiled approval. It is told of Mark Wilks, the brother of Matthew, and the grandfather of our London Mark Wilks, that when a deputation went from Norwich during the Thelwall and Horne Tooke trials, when, if the Castlereagh gang had had their will, there would have been found a short and easy way with the Dissenters, and came back on the Sunday morning, entering the place after the service had commenced, that he called out, 'What's the news?' as he saw them enter. 'Acquitted,' was the reply. 'Thank God!' said the parson, as they all joined in singing

> 'Praise God from whom all blessings flow.'

It is a fact that Wilks's first sermon in the Countess of Huntingdon's Chapel at Norwich was from the text, 'There is a lad here with five barley loaves and a few small fishes.' Let me tell another story, this time in connection with that Old Meeting which has so much to attract the visitor at Norwich. It had a grand old man, William Youngman, amongst its supporters; I see him now, with his choleric face, his full fat figure, his black knee-breeches and silk p. 199stockings, his gold-headed cane. He was an author, a learned man, as well as a Norwich merchant, the very Aristarchus of Dissent—a kind-hearted, hospitable man withal, if my boyish experience may be relied on. One Sunday there came to preach in the Old Meeting a young man named Halley from London, who lived to be honoured as few of our Dissenting D.D.'s have been. He was young, and he felt nervous as he looked from the pulpit on the austere critic in his great square pew just beneath. Well, thought the young preacher, a sermon on keeping the Sabbath will be safe, and he selected that for his morning discourse. The service over, up comes the grand old man. 'The next time, young man, you preach, preach on something you understand;' and, having said so, he bought a pennyworth of apples of a woman in the street, leaving the young man to digest his remarks as best he could. Again the service was to be carried on. The young man was in the pulpit, the grand old man below. There was singing and prayer, but no sermon, the young man having bolted after opening the service. I like better the picture of Norwich I get in Sir James Mackintosh's Life, where Basil Montague tells us how he and Mackintosh, when travelling the p. 200Norfolk circuit, always hastened to Norwich to spend their evenings in the circle of which Mrs. Taylor was the attraction and the centre. The wife of a Norwich tradesman, we see her sitting sewing and talking in the midst of her family, the companion of philosophers, who compared her to Lucy Hutchinson, and a model wife. Far away in India Sir James writes to her: 'I know the value of your letters. They rouse my mind on subjects which interest us in common—friends, children, literature, and life. Their moral tone cheers and braces me. I ought to be made permanently happy by contemplating a mind like yours; which seems more exclusively to derive its gratifications from its duties than almost any other.' It was in the Norwich Octagon that these Taylors worshipped. Their Unitarianism seemed to have affected them more favourably than it did Harriet Martineau, whose family also attended there. I remember Edward Taylor, who was the Gresham Professor of Music. But theologically, I presume, the palm of excellence in connection with the Octagon is to be awarded to Dr. Taylor, the great Hebrew scholar. He wrote to old Newton: 'I have been looking through my Bible, and can't find your doctrine of the Atonement.' 'Last night I p. 201could not see to get into bed,' replied old Newton, 'because I found I had my extinguisher on the candle. Take off the extinguisher, and then you will see.'

Leaving theology, let us get up on the gray old castle, which is to be turned into a museum, and look round on the city lying at our feet. Would you have a finer view? Cross the Yare and walk up the new road (made by the unemployed one hard winter) to Mousehold Heath, and after you have done thinking of Kitt's rebellion—an agrarian one, by-the-bye, and worth thinking about just at this time—and of the Lollards, who were burnt just under you, look across to the city in the valley, with its heights all round, more resembling the Holy City, so travellers say, than any other city in the world. In the foreground is the cathedral, right beyond rises the castle on the hill; church spires, warehouses, public buildings, private dwellings, manufactories, chimneys' smoke, complete the landscape fringed by the green of the distant hills. There are a hundred thousand people there—to be preached to and saved.

Windham was rather hard on the Norwich of his day. In his diary, in 1798, he records a visit to Norwich, of which city he was the representative. p. 202On October 9 he dined at the Swan—'dinner, like the sessions dinner, but ball in the evening distinguished by the presence of Mrs. Siddons.' On the 10th he dined at the Bishop's—'A party, of, I suppose, fifty, chiefly clergy. I felt the same enjoyment that I frequently do at large dinners—they afford, in general, what never fails to be pleasant—solitude in a crowd.' On the 11th he writes: 'Dined with sheriffs at King's Head. Robinson, the late sheriff, was there, and much as he may be below his own opinion of himself, he is more to talk to than the generality of those who are found on those occasions. I could not help reflecting on the very low state of talents or understanding in those who compose the whole, nearly, of the society of Norwich. The French are surely a more enlightened and polished people.' Perhaps Windham would have fared better had he dined with some of the leading Dissenters. Few of the clergy of East Anglia at that time would have been fitting company for the friend of Johnson and Burke. In Norwich, Mr. Windham often managed to make himself unpopular. For instance, towards the end of the session of 1788, Mr. Windham called the attention of Government to a requisition from France, which was then suffering the greatest distress p. 203from a scarcity of grain. The object of this requisition was to be supplied with 20,000 sacks of flour from this country. So small a boon ought, he thought, to be granted from motives of humanity; but a Committee of the House of Commons having decided against it, the Ministers, though they professed themselves disposed to afford the relief sought for, could not, after such a decision, undertake to grant it upon their own re-sponsibility. The leading part which Mr. Windham took in favour of this requisition occasioned, amongst some of his constituents at Norwich, considerable clamour. He allayed the storm by a private letter addressed to those citizens of Norwich who were most likely to be affected by a rise in the price of provisions; but the fact that Norwich should thus have backed up the inhuman policy of refus-ing food to France showed how strong at that time was the force of passion, and how hard it is to break down hereditary animosity. As a further illustration of manners and habits of the East Anglian cler-gy, let me mention that when, in 1778, Windham made the speech which pointed him out to be a man of marked ability in connection with the call made on the country for carrying on the American War, one of the Canons of the cathedral, and a great supporter p. 204of the war, exclaimed: 'D—n him! I could cut his tongue out!'

In my young days, in serious circles, there was no name dearer than that of Joseph Gurney—a fine-looking man with a musical voice, always ready to aid with money, or in other ways, all that was right and good, or what seemed to him such. In the 'Memorials of a Quaker Lady' he is described thus: 'He sat on the end seat of the first cross-form, and both preached and supplicated. I was very much struck with him. His fine person, his beautiful dark, glossy hair, his intelligent, benign, and truly amiable countenance, made a deep impression upon me. And as he noticed me most kindly, as I was introduced to him by Elizabeth Fry, as the little girl his sister Priscilla wanted to bring to England, I felt myself greatly honoured.'

The Gurneys have an ancient lineage, and had their home in Gourney, in Upper Normandy. One of them, of course, fought in the ranks of the winners at the battle of Hastings. Another was a crusader. Another had done good service at Acre, as a follower of Richard of the Lion Heart. When the main line came to an end, one branch settled in Norfolk. Gurney's Bank at Norwich was one of the institutions of the city, and was as famous in p. 205my day as at a later time was the great house of Overend and Gurney, which, when it fell, created a panic in financial circles all the world over.

At Earlham, the home of the Gurneys, we learn how much may be done by a family, and how widespread its influence for good or evil may become. Sir Thomas Fowell Buxton certainly stands foremost, not alone amongst the East Anglians, but the philanthropists of later years. At the age of sixteen young Buxton went to Earlham as a guest. His biographer writes: 'They received him as one of themselves, early appreciating his masterly, though still uncultivated mind; while, on his side, their cordial and encouraging welcome seemed to draw out all his latent powers. He at once joined with them in reading and study, and from this visit may be dated a remarkable change in the whole tone of his character; he received a stimulus not merely in the acquisition of knowledge, but in the formation of studious habits and intellectual tastes. Nor could the same influence fail of extending to the refinement of his disposition and manners.' At that time Norwich—the Buxtons being witnesses—was distinguished for good society, and Earlham was celebrated for its hospitality. p. 206Mr. Gurney, the father, belonged to the Society of Friends, but his family was not brought up with any strict regard to its peculiarities. He put little restraint on their domestic amusements, and music and dancing were among their favourite recreations. The third daughter, Mrs. Fry, had, indeed, united herself more closely with the Society of Friends; but her example had not then been followed by any of her brothers and sisters. 'I know,' wrote Sir Thomas, in later years, 'no blessing of a temporal nature—and it is not only temporal—for which I ought to render so many thanks as my connection with the Earlham family. It has given a colour to my life. Its influence was most positive, and pregnant with good at that critical period between school and manhood. They were eager to improve; I caught the infection. I was resolved to please them, and in the college at Dublin, at a distance from all my friends and all control, their influence and the desire to please them kept me hard at my books, and sweetened the task they gave. The distinctions I gained at college (little valuable as distinctions, but valuable because habits of industry, perseverance and resolution were necessary to attain them)—these boyish distinctions were exclusively the result of the animating p. 207passion in my mind to carry back to them the prizes which they prompted and enabled me to win.'

Wilberforce, when he was staying at Lowestoft in 1816, wrote: 'I am still full of Earlham and its excellent inhabitants. One of our great astronomers stated it as probable there may be stars whose light has been travelling to us from the Creation, and has not yet reached our little planet. In the Earlham family a new constellation has broken in upon us, for which you must invent a name, as you are fond of star-gazing, and if it indicates a little monstrosity (as they are apt to give the collection of stars the names of strange creatures—dragons, bears, etc.), the various stars of which the Earlham assemblage is made,' continues Wilberforce, 'will include also much to be respected and loved.' At that time Mrs. Opie was one of the Norwich stars. Caroline Fox, who went to dine with her described her as in great force and really jolly. 'She is enthusiastic about Father Mathew, reads Dickens voraciously, takes to Carlyle, but thinks his appearance rather against him—talks much and with great spirit of people, but never ill-naturedly.'

'Norwich,' as described by Camden, 'on account of its wealth, populousness, neatness of buildings, p. 208beautiful churches, with the number of them—for it has a matter of fifty parishes—as also the industry of its citizens, loyalty to their Prince, is to be reckoned among the most considerable cities in Britain. It was fortified with walls that have a great many turrets and eleven gates.' Camden, quoting one writer after another, adds the eulogy of Andrew Johnston, a Scotchman, as follows:

> 'A town whose stately piles and happy seat
> Her citizens and strangers both delight;
> Whose tedious siege and plunder made her bear
> In Norman battles an unhappy share,

And feel the sad effects of dreadful war.
These storms o'erblown, now blest with constant
peace,
She saw her riches and her trade increase.
State here by wealth, by beauty yet undone,
How blest if vain excess be yet unknown!
So fully is she from herself supplied
That England while she stands can never want a
head.'

From Norwich went Robinson to help to build up in Amsterdam that Church of the Pilgrim Fathers which was to be in its turn the mother of a great Republic such as the world had never seen. He has been styled the Father of Modern Congregationalism; be that as it may, when he bade farewell in that quaint old harbour, Delfhaven—which looks as if not a brick or a building had been touched since—he was doing a work from which p. 209neither himself nor those who stood with him could ever have expected such wonderful results. That emigration to Holland in Wren's time was a great loss of money and men to England, and was an indication of Nonconformist strength which wise Churchmen would have conciliated rather than driven to extremities. 'In sooth it was,' wrote Heylin, 'that the people in many great trading towns which were near the sea, having long been discharged of the bond of ceremonies, no sooner came to hear the least noise of a conformity, but they began to spurn against it; and when they found that all their striving was in vain, that they had lost the comfort of their lecturers and that their ministers began to shrink at the very name of a visitation, it was no hard matter for those ministers and lecturers to persuade them to remove their dwellings and transport their trades.' 'The sun of heaven,' say they, 'doth shine as comfortably in other places; the Sun of Righteousness much brighter.' 'Better to go and dwell in Goshen, find it where we can, than tarry in the midst of such an Egyptian darkness as is now falling on the land.' One of the preachers who gave that advice and acted in accordance with it was William Bridge, M.A. Against him Wren p. 210was so furious that he fled to Holland and settled down as one of the pastors of the church at Rotterdam. In 1643 we find him pastor of the church at Norwich and Yarmouth, and one of the Assembly of Divines. In 1644 the church was separated—a part meeting at Yarmouth and a part at Norwich. This was done on the advice of Mr. John Phillip, of Wrentham—a godly minister of great influence in his denomination in his day.

As was to be expected, I was taken to the Old Meeting House at Norwich, where many learned men had preached, and where many men almost as learned listened. The gigantic pews, in which a small family might have lived, filled me with amazement. And equally appalling to me was the respectability of the people, of a very different class from that of our Wrentham chapel. Close by was the Octagon Chapel, where the Unitarians worshipped, equally impressive in its respectability. But what struck me most was the new and fashionable Baptist chapel of St. Mary's, where the venerable and learned Kinghorn preached—a great Hebrew scholar and the champion of strict communion—against Robert Hall, and other degenerate Baptists, who were ready to admit to the Lord's Table any Christians, whether properly p. 211baptized—that is, by immersion when adults—or merely sprinkled as infants. Up to this day I confound the worthy man with John the Baptist, probably because he looked so lank and long and lean. He was a man of singularly precise habits, so much so that I heard of an old lady who always regulated her cooking by his daily walk, putting the dumplings into the pot to boil when he went, and taking them out when he returned. I could write much about him, but *cui bono*? who cares about a dead Baptist lion? Not even the Baptists themselves. On going into their library in Castle Street the other day, to look at Kinghorn's life, I found no one had taken the trouble to cut the pages. In the front gallery of St. Mary's, Mr. Brewer, the Norwich schoolmaster, had sittings for the boys of his school, including his own sons, who, at King's College and elsewhere, have done much to illustrate our national history and literature. If I remember aright, one of the congregation was a jolly-looking old gentleman who, as Uncle Jerry, laid the foundation of a mustard manufactory, which has placed one of the present M.P.'s for Norwich at the head of a business of unrivalled extent. When Mr. Kinghorn died, his place was taken by Mr. Brock, better known as Dr. Brock, p. 212of Bloomsbury Chapel, London. Under Mr. Brock's preaching the reputation of St. Mary's Chapel was increased rather than diminished. As a young man himself at that time, he was peculiarly attractive to the young, and the singing was very different from the rustic psalmody of my native village, in spite of the fact that we had a bass-viol at all times, and on highly-favoured occasions such an array of flutes and clarionets as really astonished the natives and delighted me.

But to return to the Old Meeting. Calamy writes of one of the Norwich ministers, of the name of Cromwell, that 'he enjoyed but one peaceable day after his settlement, being on the second forced out of his meeting-house, the licenses being called in, and then for nine years together he was never without trouble. Sometimes he was pursued with indictments at sessions, at assizes, and then with citations of the ecclesiastical courts; and at other times feigned letters, rhymes or libels were dropped in the streets or church and fathered upon him, so that he was forced to make his house his prison. At length that was broken open, and he absconded into the houses of his friends, till he contracted his old disease' a second time. It is said that he was invited on one occasion to dine with Bishop Reynolds, p. 213when several young clergy were present. When Mr. Cromwell retired, the Bishop rose and attended him, and then a general laugh ensued. On his return his lordship rebuked his guests for their unmannerly conduct, and told them that Mr. Cromwell had more solid divinity in his little finger than all of them had in their bodies. It must be remembered that, like most of the early Independent ministers, Mr. Cromwell had a University training; and even in my young days the respect shown to a learned ministry kept up not a little of the high standard which had been laid down by the fathers and founders of Dissent. In these more degenerate days it is to be questioned whether as much can be said. The Old Meeting House at Norwich was finished as far back as 1643. The only pastor of the church who was not an author was the Rev. Dr. Scott, who died in 1767. In the Octagon Chapel the preachers had been still more distinguished. One of them was the Rev. Dr. Taylor, author of the famous Hebrew Concordance, which was published in two volumes folio, and was the labour of fourteen years. He left Norwich to become tutor at the newly-erected Academy at Warrington; but his son, Mr. Edward Taylor, the Gresham Professor of Music, was often p. 214a visitor at Wrentham, where he had a little property, which he valued, as it gave him a vote. Another of the preachers at the Octagon was the Rev. R. Alderson, who afterwards became Recorder of Norwich. The Mr. Edward Taylor of whom I have just written was baptized by him. One day, being under examination as a witness in court, Alderson questioned him as to his age. 'Why,' said Taylor, a little nettled, 'you ought to know, for you baptized me.' 'I baptized you!' exclaimed Alderson. 'What do you mean?' The Recorder never liked to be reminded of his having been a preacher. The Marchioness of Salisbury is of this family. Perhaps, of these Unitarian preachers, one of the most distinguished was Dr. William Enfield, whose 'Speaker' was one of the books placed in the hands of ingenuous youth, and whose 'History of Philosophy' was one of the works to be studied in their riper years. Norwich, indeed, was full of learned men. Its aged Bishop, Bathurst, was the one voter for Reform, much to the delight of William IV., who said that he was a fine fellow, and deserved to be the helmsman of the Church in the rough sea she would soon have to steer through. His one offence in the eyes of George III. was that he voted against the King—that is, in favour p. 215of justice to the Catholics. With such a Bishop a Reformer, no wonder that all Norwich went wild with joy when the battle of Reform was fought and won. Bishop Stanley, who succeeded, was also in his way a great Liberal, and invited Jenny Lind to stay with him at the palace. I often used to see him at Exeter Hall, where his activity as a speaker afforded a remarkable contrast to the quieter style of his more celebrated son.

Accidentally looking into the life of Bishop Bathurst, I find printed in the Appendix some interesting conversations at Earlham, where Joseph John Gurney lived. On one occasion, when Dr. Chalmers was staying there, Joseph John Gurney writes: 'W. Y. breakfasted with us, and with his usual strong sense and talent called forth the energies of Chalmers' mind. They conversed on the subject of special Providence, and of the unseen yet unceasing superintendence of the Creator of all the events which occur in this lower world. Said W. Y.: "Mr. Barbauld, the husband of the authoress, was once a resident in my house. He was a man of low opinions in religion, and denied the agency of an unseen spirit on the mind of man." I remarked that when the mind was determined to a certain right action by a combination of circumstances p.

216productive of the adequate motives, and meeting from various quarters precisely at the right point for the purpose in view, this was in itself a sufficient evidence of an especial Providence, and might be regarded as the instrumentality through which the Holy Spirit acts. Mr. Barbauld admitted the justice of this argument.' Again I read: 'W. Y. supported the doctrine that nature is governed through the means of general laws — laws which broadly and obviously mark the wisdom and benevolence of God.' One extract more: 'W. Y. expressed his admiration of the masterly manner in which Dr. Chalmers, in his "Bridgewater Treatise," has fixed on the atheist a moral obligation to inquire into the truth of religion; but, said he, might not the disciples of Irving, by the same rule, oblige us to an inquiry into the supposed evidences of their favourite doctrine that Christ is about to appear and to reign personally on earth? Might not even the Mahometan suppose in the Christian a similar necessity as it relates to the pretensions of the false prophet?' If Joseph Gurney sent for W. Y. to converse with Dr. Chalmers as a genial spirit, surely the name of one so honourable and of one so friendly both to my father and myself should not be omitted. W. Y. loved a joke. He was p. 217very stout, and wore tight black knee breeches with shoes and silk stockings. I remember how he made me laugh one day as he described what happened to his knee-breeches as he stooped to tie up his shoes ere attending a place of worship. To cut a long story short, I may add W. Youngman did not go to church that day. Originally I think he was a dyer.

Harriet Martineau, as all the world knows, was born at Norwich. In her somewhat ill-natured autobiography she writes: 'Norwich, which has now no social claims to superiority at all, was in my childhood a rival of Lichfield itself, in the time of the Sewards, for literary pretensions and the vulgarity of pedantry. William Taylor was then at his best, when there was something like fulfilment of his early promise, when his exemplary filial duty was a fine spectacle to the whole city, and before the vice which destroyed him had coarsened his morale and destroyed his intellect. During the war it was a great distinction to know anything of German literature, and in Mr. Taylor's case it proved a ruinous distinction. He was completely spoiled by the flatteries of shallow men, pedantic women, and conceited lads.' Yet this man was the friend of Southey and opened up a p. 218new world to the English intellect, and perhaps in days to come will have a more enduring reputation than Harriet Martineau herself. The lady does not err on the side of good nature in her criticism. All she can say of Dr. Sayers is: 'I always heard of him as a genuine scholar, and I have no doubt he was superior to his neighbours in modesty and manners. Dr. Enfield, a feeble and superficial man of letters, was gone also from the literary supper-table before my time. There was Sir James Smith, the botanist, made much of and really not pedantic and vulgar like the rest, but weak and irritable. There was Dr. Alderson, Mrs. Opie's father, solemn and sententious and eccentric in manner, but not an able man in any way;' and thus the leading lights of Norwich are contemptuously dismissed. 'The great days of the Gurneys were not come yet. The remarkable family from which issued Mrs. Fry and Priscilla and Joseph John Gurney were then a set of dashing young people, dressed in gay riding habits and scarlet boots, as Mrs. Fry told us afterwards, and riding about the country to balls and gaieties of all sorts. Accomplished and charming young ladies they were; and we children used to overhear some whispered gossip about the effects of their charms p. 219on heart-stricken young men; but their final characteristics were not yet apparent.'

It is to a Norwich man that we owe the publication of Hansard's Parliamentary Debates. Luke Hansard, to whom they owe their name, was born in Norwich, 1725, was trained as a printer, went to London with but a guinea in his pocket, was employed by Hughes, the printer of the House of Commons, succeeded to the business and became widely known for his despatch and accuracy in print-ing Parliamentary papers and debates. He died in 1828, but the business was continued by his family, and to refer to Hansard be-came the invariable custom when an M.P. was to be condemned out of his own mouth — as Hansard was supposed never to err. Recently Hansard has been carried on by a company, but the old name still remains.

Dr. Stoughton has in vain, in a number of the *Congregationalist*, at-tempted to record the memory of a man well known and much honoured in his day — the Rev. John Alexander, of Norwich. The portrait is a failure. It gives us no idea of the man with his rosy face, his curly black hair, his merry, twinkling eye, his joyous laugh, when mirth befitted the occasion, or his tender sympathy p. 220where pain and sorrow and distress had to be endured. Mr. Alexander's jubilee was celebrated in St. Andrew's Hall in 1867, when the Mayor and a crowd of citizens did him honour, and a sum of money for the purchase of an annuity was presented, thus obviating the necessity of doing to him as on one occasion he in his humorous way suggested should be done with old ministers when past work—that they should be shot. In 1817 Mr. Alexander had come to Norwich to preach in the old Whitfield Tabernacle in place of Mr. Hooper, one of the tutors at Hoxton Academy. When I went to Norwich he had built a fine chapel in Prince's Street, and amongst the hearers was Mr. Tillet, then in a lawyer's office, a young man famous for his speeches at the Mechanics' Institute and in connection with a literary venture, the *Norwich Magazine*, not destined to set the Thames on fire; latterly an M.P. for Norwich and proprietor and editor, I believe, of one of the most popular of East Anglian journals, the *Norfolk News*. It was in Prince's Street Chapel I first learned to realize how influential was the Nonconformist public, of which I frankly admit in our little village, with Churchmen all round, I had but a limited idea. It seemed to me that we were rather a puny folk, p. 221but at Norwich, with its chapels and pastors and people, I saw another sight. There was the Rev. John Alexander, with an overflowing audience on the Sunday and an active vitality all the week, now dining at the palace with the Bishop or breakfasting at Earlham with the Gurneys, now meeting on terms of equality the literati of the place (at that time Mrs. Opie was still living near the castle, and Mr. Wilkins was writing his life of the far-famed Norwich doctor, the learned and ingenious author of the 'Religio Medici'), now visiting the afflicted and the destitute, now carrying consolation to the home of the mourner. John Alexander was a man to whom East Anglian Nonconformity owes much. In the old city there was a good deal of young intelligence, and a good deal of it amongst the Noncons. Dr. Sexton was one of the Old Meeting House congregation, as was Lucy Brightwell, a lady not unknown to the present generation of readers. To a certain extent a Noncon. is bound to be more or less intelligent. He finds a great State Establishment of religion wherever he goes. It enjoys the favour of the Court. It is patronized by the aristocracy. It enlists among its supporters all who wish to rise in the world or to make a figure in society. By means of the endowed p. 222schools of the land, it offers to the young, even of the humblest birth, a chance of winning a prize. Conform, it says, and you may be rich and respectable. It was said of a late Bishop of Winchester that he would forgive a man anything so long as he were but a good Churchman, and even now one meets in society with people who regard a Dissenter as little better than a heathen or a publican. A man who can thus voluntarily place himself at a disadvantage, to a certain extent, must have exercised his intellect and be ready to give a reason for the faith that is in him. Naturally, men are of the religion of the country in which they are born—Roman Catholics in Italy, Mahometans in Turkey, Buddhists in the East. It requires more power and strength of mind and decision of character to dissent from the Church of the State than to support it. 'How was it,' asked Dr. Storrar, Chairman of the Convocation of the University of London, the other day, 'that the lads educated at Mill Hill Grammar School had done so well at Cambridge and Oxford?' The reply, said the Doctor, was—I don't give his words, merely the idea—to be found in the fact that a couple of centuries ago there were men of strong intellect and tender consciences who refused p. 223to renounce their opinions at the command of a despotic power. They had been succeeded by their sons with the same quickness of intellect and conscience. Generations one after another had come and gone, and the children of these old Nonconformists thus came to the school with an hereditary intelligence, destined to win in the gladiatorship of the school, the college, or the world.

Let me now give an anecdote of Dr. Bathurst, the Lord Bishop of Norwich, too good to be lost. It is told by Sir Charles Leman, who described him in 1839 as gradually converting his enemies into friends by his uniform straightforwardness and enlarged Christian principle. One of his clergy, who had been writing most abusively in newspapers, had on one occasion some favour to solicit, which he did with natural hesitation. The Bishop promised all in his power and in the kindest manner, and when the clergyman was about to leave the room he suddenly turned with, 'My lord, I must say, however, I much regret the part I have taken against you; I see I was quite in the wrong, and I beg your forgiveness.' This was readily accorded. 'But how was it,' the clergyman continued, 'you did not turn your back on p. 224me? I quite expected it.' 'Why, you forget that I profess myself a Christian,' was the reply.

Of a later Bishop—Stanley—whom I can well remember, a dark, energetic little man, making a speech at Exeter Hall, we hear a little in Caroline Fox's memories of old friends. In 1848 she writes: 'Dined very pleasantly at the palace; the Bishop was all animation and good humour, but too unsettled to leave any memorable impression. I like Mrs. Stanley much—a shrewd, sensible, observing woman. She told me much about her Bishop, how very trying his position was on first settling at Norwich; for his predecessor was an amiable, indolent old man, who let things take their course, and a very bad course too, all which the present man has to correct as way opens, and continually sacrifice popularity to a sense of right.'

The following anecdote of Miss Fox and her friends calling at a cottage in the neighbourhood of Norwich is too good to be lost. 'A young woman,' she writes, 'told us that her father was nearly converted, and that a little more teaching would complete the business,' adding, 'He quite believes that he is lost, which is, of course, a great consolation to the old man.' That story is racy of the soil. It is in that way the East Anglian peasantry p. 225who have any religion at all talk; they have no hope of a man who does not feel that he is lost. Well, there are many ways to heaven, and that must comfort some of us who still believe that man was made in the image of his Maker, a little lower than the angels, crowned with glory and honour, and not destined to an eternity of misery for the sins of a day.

p. 226CHAPTER VIII.
the suffolk capital.

The Orwell — The Sparrows — Ipswich notabilities — Gainsborough — Medical men — Nonconformists.

Those who imagine Suffolk to be a flat and uninteresting county, with no charms for the eye and no associations worth speaking of, are much mistaken. There are few lovelier rivers in England than the Orwell, on which Ipswich stands, up which river the fiery Danes used to sail to plunder all the country round, and on the banks of which Gainsborough learned to love Nature and draw her in all her charms. The town itself stands in a valley, but it has gradually crept up the hills on each side, so that almost everywhere you have a pleasing prospect and breathe a bracing air. A few miles, or, rather, a short walk, brings you to Henley, which has the reputation of being the highest land in Suffolk, and on the other side there is a railway that connects Ipswich with Felixstowe, p. 227just as the Crystal Palace is connected with the City. Ipswich may claim to be the most prosperous and enterprising of all the Suffolk towns. It goes with the times. Its citizens are active and pushing men of business, and have enlightened ideas as well. They are also Liberal in politics and practical in religion, and are never behind in coming forward when there is a chance of benefiting themselves or their fellow-creatures. And yet Ipswich has a history as long as the dullest cathedral town. It was a place of note during the existence of the Saxon Heptarchy. Twice it had the honour of publicly entertaining King John; and there is a tradition that in the curious and beautifully-ornamented house in the Butter Market — formerly the residence of Mr. Sparrow, the Ipswich coroner, whose old family portraits, including one of the Jameses, presented to an ancestor of the family, filled me not a little with youthful wonder — Charles II. was secreted by one of the Sparrows of that day, when he came to hide in Ipswich after the battle of Worcester. 'The house is now a shop,' but, observes Mr. Glyde, a far-famed local historian, 'a concealed room in the upper story of the house, which was discovered during some alterations in 1801, is well adapted for such a p. 228purpose.' And, at any rate, the gay and graceless monarch, in search of a hiding-place, might have gone farther and fared worse. Be that as it may, Ipswich can rejoice in the fact that it was the birthplace of Cardinal Wolsey; and that he was one of the first educational reformers of the day must be admitted, at any rate, in Ipswich, of which, possibly, he would have made a second Cambridge. Alas! of his efforts in that direction, the only outward and visible sign is the old gateway in what is called College Street, which remains to this day. Ipswich fared well in the Elizabethan days, when her Gracious Majesty condescended to visit the place. Sir Christopher Hatton, the dancing Lord Chancellor, who led the brawls, when

'The seals and maces danced before him,'

lived in a house near the Church of St. Mary-le-Tower. Sir Edward Coke resided in a village not far off, and in 1597 the M.P. for Ipswich was no other than the great Lord Bacon, who by birth and breeding was emphatically a Suffolk man. From Windham's diary, it appears that at Ipswich that distinguished statesman experienced a new sensation. In 1789 he writes: 'Left Ipswich not till near twelve. Saw Humphries there, and p. 229was for the first time entertained with some sparring; felt much amused with the whole of the business.'

In the early part of the present century Miss Berry, on returning from one of her Continental trips, paid Ipswich a visit, having landed at Southwold. 'Appearance of Ipswich very pretty in descending towards it,' is the entry in her diary. About the same time Bishop Bathurst made his visitation tour, and he writes to one of his lady correspondents: 'You will be glad that, during the three weeks I passed in Suffolk, I did not meet a single unpleasant man, nor experience a single unpleasant accident.' With the name of the Suffolk hero Captain Broke, of the *Shannon*. (I can well remember the Shannon coach—which ran from Yoxford to London—the only day-coach we had at that time), Ipswich is inseparably connected. He was born at Broke Hall, just by, and there spent the later years of his life. Another of our naval heroes, Admiral Vernon, the victor of Porto Bello, resided in the same vicinity. At one time there seems to have been an attempt to connect Ipswich with the Iron Duke. In the memoir of Admiral Broke we have more than one reference to the Duke's shooting in that neighbourhood, p. 230and actually it appears that, unknown to himself, he was nominated as a candidate to the office of High Steward. Ipswich, however, preferred a neighbour, in the shape of Sir Robert Harland. At a later day the office was filled by Mr. Charles Austin, the distinguished writer on Jurisprudence.

One of the celebrated noblemen who lived in Ipswich was Lord Chedworth. He wore top-boots, and wore them till they were not fit to be seen. When new boots were sent home he was accustomed to set them on one side, and get his manservant to wear them a short time to prepare them for his own feet. Sometimes the man would tell his lordship that he thought the boots were ready, but his lordship would generally reply, 'Never mind, William; wear them another week.' While at Ipswich his lordship was frequently consulted, owing to his legal attainments and well-known generous disposition, by tradesmen and people in indigent circumstances. The applicants were ushered into the library, where, surrounded by books, they found his lordship. The chairs and furniture of the room, like his lordship's clothes, had not merely seen their best days, but were comparatively worthless, and the old red cloak which invariably enveloped his shoulders made him look p. 231more like a gipsy boy than a peer of the realm. His lordship's legacies to Ipswich ladies and others, especially of the theatrical profession, were of the most liberal character.

Ipswich in its old days had its share of witches. One of the most notorious of them was Mother Hatheland, who in due course was tried, condemned and executed. From her confession in 1645 it appears 'the said Mother Hatheland hath been a professor of religion, a constant hearer of the Word for these many years, yet a witch, as she confessed, for the space of nearly twenty years. The devil came to her first between sleeping and waking, and spake to her in a hollow voice, telling her that if she would serve him she would want nothing. After often solicitations she consented to him. Then he stroke his claw (as she confessed) into her hands, and with her blood wrote the covenant.' Now, as the writer gravely remarks, the subtlety of Satan is to be observed in that he did not press her to deny God and Christ, as he did others, because she was a professor, and he might have lost all his hold by pressing her too far. Satan appears to have provided her with three imps, in the shape of two little dogs and a mole.

p. 232As the home of Gainsborough Ipswich has enduring claims on the English nation and on lovers of art and artists everywhere. That must have been a Suffolk man who passed the following criticism on Gainsborough's celebrated picture of 'Girl and Pigs,' of which Sir Joshua Reynolds became the purchaser at one hundred guineas, though the artist asked but sixty: 'They be deadly like pigs; but who ever saw pigs feeding together, but one on 'em had a foot in the trough?' Gainsborough had an enthusiastic attachment to music. It was the favourite amusement of his leisure hours, and his love for it induced him to give one or two concerts to his most intimate acquaintances whilst living in Ipswich. He was a member of a musical club, and painted some of the portraits of his brother members in his picture of a choir. Once upon a time, Gainsborough was examined as a witness on a trial respecting the originality of a picture. The barrister on the other side said: 'I observe you lay great stress on a painter's eye; what do you mean by that expression?' 'A painter's eye,' replied Gainsborough, 'is to him what the lawyer's eye is to you.' As a boy at the Grammar School of his native town, it is to be feared he loved to play truant. One day he went out to his p. 233usual sketching haunts to enjoy the nature which he loved heartily, previously presenting to his uncle, who was master of the school, the usual slip of paper, 'Give Tom a holiday,' in which his father's handwriting was so exactly imitated that not the slightest suspicion of the forgery ever entered the mind of the master. Alas! however, the crime was detected, and his terrified parent exclaimed in despair, 'Tom will one day be hanged.' When, however, he was informed how the truant schoolboy had employed his truant hours, and the boy's sketches were laid before him, forgetful of the consequences of forgeries in a commercial society, he declared, with all the pride of a father, 'Tom will be a genius,' and he was right.

Worthy Mr. Pickwick seems to have known Ipswich about the same time as myself. 'In the main street of Ipswich,' wrote the biographer of that distinguished individual, 'on the left-hand side of the way, a short distance after you have passed through the open space fronting the Town Hall, stands an inn known far and wide by the appellation of the Great White Horse, rendered the more conspicuous by a stone statue of some rapacious animal, with flowing mane and tail, distantly p. 234resembling an insane carthorse, which is elevated above the principal door. The Great White Horse is famous in the neighbourhood in the same degree as a prize ox, a county paper chronicled turnip, or unwieldy pig, for its enormous size. Never were such labyrinths of uncarpeted passages, such clusters of mouldy, ill-lighted rooms, such huge numbers of small dens for eating or sleeping in, beneath any one roof as are collected together between the four walls of the Great White Horse of Ipswich.' This was the great hotel of the Ipswich of my youth. As regards hotels, Ipswich has not improved, but in every other way it has much advanced. One of the old inns has been turned into a fine public hall, admirably adapted for concerts and public meetings. The new Town Hall, Corn Exchange, and Post-office are a credit to the town. The same may be said of the new Museum and the Grammar School and the Working Men's College and that health resort, the Arboretum; while by means of the new dock ships of fifteen hundred tons burden can load and unload. Nowadays everybody says Ipswich is a rising town, and what everyone says must be right. The Ipswich people, at any rate, have firmly got that idea into their heads. Its fathers and founders p. 235built the streets narrow, evidently little anticipating for Ipswich the future it has since achieved. The Ipswich of to-day is laid out on quite a different scale. It has a tram road service evidently much in excess of the present population, and as you wander in the suburbs you come to a sign-post bearing the name of a street in which not even the enterprise of the speculative builder has been able at present to plant a single dwelling. When Ipswich has climbed up its surrounding hills, and taken up all the building sites at present in the market, it will be a goodly and gallant town, almost fitted to invite the temporary residence of holiday-making Londoners who are fond of the water. At all times it is a pretty sail to Harwich and thence to Felixstowe, that quiet watering-place, a seaside residence that has still a pleasant flavour of rusticity about it, with a fine crisp sea-sand floor for a promenade.

When I was a boy Ipswich was resorted to by Londoners in the summer-time. As an illustration, I give the case of Mr. Ewen, one of the deacons of the Weigh House Chapel, when the Rev. John Clayton was the pastor. In his memories of the Clayton family, the Rev.

Dr. Aveling writes of Mr. Ewen, that 'he was so sensitively conscientious p. 236in the discharge of his official duties at the Weigh House, that he was never absent from town on the days when the Lord's Supper was administered, and when he was expected to assist in the administration of the elements. His London residence was in Lincoln's Inn Fields, but having a house and property in the town of Ipswich, he passed his summer months there. Yet so intent was he upon duly filling his place in the sanctuary of God, that he regularly travelled by post-chaise once in every month, and returned in the same manner, that he might be present, together with his pastor and the brethren, at the table of the Lord. The length and the expense of the journey (and travelling was not then what it is now) did not deter him from what he at least deemed to be a matter of Christian obligation.' Dr. Aveling is quite right when he tells us travelling is not what it was. It took almost a day to go from Ipswich to London when I was a boy, and now the journey is done by means of the Great Eastern Railway in about an hour and a half. It seems marvellous to one who, like myself, remembers well the past, to leave Liverpool Street at 5.0 p.m. precisely, and to find one's self landed safe and well in Ipswich soon after half-past six. The present generation can p. 237have no conception of travelling in England in the olden time.

There were some wonderful old Radicals in Ipswich, though it was, and is, the county town of the most landlord-ridden district in England. Some of them got the great Dan O'Connell to pay the town a visit, and some of them nobly stood by old John Childs when he became famous all the world over as the Church-rate martyr. The lawyers and the doctors were mostly Tories, but the tradesmen and the merchants were not a little leavened with the leaven of Dissent. Mr. Hammond was, however, a Liberal surgeon, and as such flourished. His Whig principles, writes Mr. Glyde, brought him many patients, and his skill and sound qualities retained them. Dr. Garrord, the well-known London practitioner, was an apprentice of Mr. Hammond's; and this reminds me that among the Ipswich men who have risen is Mr. Sprigg, the Premier of Cape Colony when Sir Bartle Frere was at the head of affairs there. The father of Mr. Sprigg was the respected pastor of a Baptist chapel in the town. The only Ipswich minister whom I can remember was the Rev. Mr. Notcutt, who preached in the leading Independent chapel, now pulled down to make way for a much more p. 238attractive building. All I can recollect about him is, that once, when a lad, I fainted away when he was preaching. No sermon ever affected me so since; and that effect was due, it must be confessed, not to the preacher, who seemed to me rather aged and asthmatic, but to the heat of the place, in consequence of the crowd attracted to the meeting-house on some special occasion.

But to return to the doctors. Of one of them, who was famed for his love of bleeding his patients, not metaphorically, but in the old-fashioned way, with the lancet, it is recorded that on the occasion of his taking a holiday two of his patients died. Lamenting the fact to a friend, the following epigram was the result:

'B--- kills two patients while from home away —
A clever fellow this same B---, I wot;
If absent thus his patients he can slay,
How he must kill them when he's on the spot!'

Perhaps one of the noted physicians of my boyhood was Mr. Stebbing. 'He was once,' writes Mr. Glyde, 'called in to see one of the Ipswich Dissenting ministers, who had taken life very easily, and had grown corpulent. After examining the patient and hearing his statement as to bodily state, he replied: "You've no particular ailment; p. 239mind and keep your eyes longer open, and your mouth longer shut, and you will do very well in a short time."' On another occasion a raw and very poor-looking young fellow called upon him for advice. The doctor told him to go home and eat more pudding, adding, 'That's all you want; physic is a very good thing for one to live by, but a precious bad thing for you to take.' One of the Ipswich characters of my boyhood, of whom Mr. Glyde has preserved an anecdote, was old Tuxford, the veterinary surgeon. He used to declare that he never took more than one meal a day — a breakfast; but when asked of what that consisted, he said, 'A pound of beefsteak, seven eggs, three cups of tea, and a quartern of rum.' It may also be mentioned that before Mrs. Garrett Anderson was born, Ipswich had a lady physician in the person of Miss Stebbing, daughter of the doctor to whom I have already referred. 'She was,' says one who knew her well, 'a woman of general education, with more than ordinary tact and discernment, combined with the true womanly power of analyzing and observing. She had good physical powers, and, like her worthy father, was somewhat pungent in her remarks and eccentric in her habits. She entered the ranks as a medical practitioner during her father's life. The p. 240benefit of his advice so aided her perceptive powers as to make her quite an expert in various ways, and she continued to practise long after his decease, occasionally attending males as well as females. Her knowledge of midwifery caused a large number of ladies to engage her services.

Of the Radicals of Ipswich, the only one with whom I came into contact was Mr. John King, the proprietor and editor of what was then, at any rate, a far-famed journal—the *Suffolk Chronicle*. Astronomy was his hobby, and he had ideas on the subject which, unfortunately, I failed to catch. He had built himself an observatory, if I remember aright, at his residence on Rose Hill, where he would sweep the heavens nightly, to see what could be seen. He was a Radical of the old type, a tall, dark, bilious-looking man, a little hard and dry, perhaps, who seemed to think that it was no use to throw pearls before swine, and to serve up for the chaw-bacons a too rich intellectual treat, and his policy was a successful one. Priest-ridden as Suffolk was, the *Suffolk Chronicle* was the leading paper of the county, and had a large circulation, and, let me add, did good service in its day. Now I find Ipswich rejoices in a well-conducted daily journal, the *East Anglian Times*, which I hear, and p. 241am glad to hear, is a fine property, and I see all the leading towns in Suffolk have a paper to themselves, even if they can't get up a decent paragraph of local news—and some of them I know, from my experiences of Suffolk life, are quite unequal to that—once a week. The plan is to have some sheets already printed in London, at some great establishment, whence perhaps a hundred little towns are supplied, and then the local news and advertisements are added on, and Little Pedlington has its *Observer*, and Eatanswill its *Gazette*. When I was a boy, such a thing was out of the question, as to each paper a fourpenny-halfpenny stamp was attached. As the stamps had to be paid for in advance, and as, besides, there was an eighteen-penny duty on every advertisement, it was not quite such an easy matter to run a paper then as it has since become. I fancy the

144

old-established journals suffered much by the change, which completely revolutionized the newspaper trade; at any rate, so far as the country was concerned. In this connection, let me add that it was to an Ipswich journalist we owe the establishment of penny readings on anything like a large and successful scale. They were originated by Mr. Sully, at that time the proprietor and editor of the *Ipswich* p. 242 *Express*, a paper intended to steer between the ferocious Toryism of the *Ipswich Journal,* and the equally ferocious Radicalism of the *Suffolk Chronicle*. As was to be expected, the attempt did not succeed. As in love and in war, so in politics and theology, moderation is a thing hateful to gods and men. The electioneering annals of Ipswich can testify to that fact. I have a dim recollection of an election petition which ended in Sir Fitzroy Kelly's admitting that he had stated what was not true, but he did it as a lawyer, not as a gentleman, and in sending one of the finest old gentlemen I ever knew to gaol, because he would not tell what he knew of the matter. There was not much half-and-half work in the Ipswich politics of my young days.

When people fight fiercely in politics, it is natural to expect an equal earnestness in religious matters. It was so emphatically with respect to the Ipswich of the past. 'The Reformed religion, after those fiery days of persecution,' writes John Quick, 'was now revived, and flourished again in the country, under the auspicious name of our English Deborah, Queen Elizabeth; and Ipswich, the capital town of Suffolk, was not more famous for its spacious sheds, large and beautiful buildings, rich and great trade, p. 243and honourable merchants, both at home and abroad, than it was for its learned and godly ministers and its religious intolerants.' Of the godly ministers, one of the most famous was Samuel Ward, who was buried in St. Mary-le-Tower Church. In 1666 he preached a sermon at St. Paul's Cross. But he meddled with politics. For instance, in 1621 he published a caricature picture, entitled 'Spayne and Rome Defeated.' It is thus described: The Pope and his Council are represented in the centre of the piece, and beneath, on one side the Armada, and on the other the Gunpowder Treason. Gondomar, the Spanish Ambassador, complained of it as insulting to his master. Ward was placed in custody. Being Puritanically inclined, he was, in addition, prosecuted in the Consistory Court of Norwich by

Bishop Harsnet for Nonconformity. Ten years later, when 600 persons were contemplating a removal from Ipswich to New England — as a place where they could worship God without fear of priest or king — the blame was cast by Laud on Ward. Rushworth informs us that the charges laid against him were that he preached against the common bowing at the name of Jesus and against the King's 'Book of Sports,' and further said that p. 244the Church of England was ready to ring changes in England, and that the Gospel stood on tiptoe as ready to be gone; and for this he was removed from his lectureship and sent to gaol. John Ward, his brother, Rector of St. Clement's, was a member of the Assembly of Divines, and was called to preach two sermons before the House of Commons, for which he received the thanks of the House. At that time we find a reference to Ipswich as a place which 'the Lord hath long made famous and happy as a valley of Gospel vision.' Such places, alas! seem to have been commoner formerly than they are now.

One of the Congregational churches of Ipswich, at any rate, has very interesting historical associations. 'Salem Chapel,' writes the Rev. John Browne, in his 'History of Congregationalism in Suffolk and Norfolk,' 'stands in St. George's Lane, opposite the place where St. George's Chapel formerly stood, where Bilney was apprehended when preaching in favour of the Reformation, and where he so enraged the monks that they twice plucked him out of the pulpit.' The last time I was at Ipswich I saw bricklayers at work at the old Presbyterian church in St. Nicholas Street, which it would be a pity to see modernized, being p. 245such a fine illustration of the old-fashioned Dissenting Meeting-house, before it became the fashion to have a taste and to build Gothic chapels in which it is difficult to see or hear, and the only advantage of which is that they are an exact copy of the steeple-houses against which at one time Nonconformist England waged remorseless war. One of the pastors of this congregation removed to Mill Hill Chapel, Leeds, where he succeeded Dr. Priestley; another was the author of a 'History and Description of Derbyshire'; while one of the supplies was the Rev. Robert Alderson, afterwards of the Octagon Chapel, Norwich, who ultimately became a lawyer and Recorder of Norwich. Perhaps one of the most singular scenes connected with Dissenting chapels in Ipswich was that which took place in the old chapel in Tackard, now Tacket,

Street. In 1766 the minister there was the Rev. Mr. Edwards, who, it appears, was sent for to the gaol to see two men who had been found guilty of house-breaking, and who, according to the law as it then stood, were to be hung. Mr. Edwards did so, and stayed with them two hours. As the result of this visit they were brought to a penitent state of mind. They had heard that Mr. Edwards had prepared a sermon for them and p. 246desired them to attend. This was a mistake, but notwithstanding they obtained permission to go to the chapel, where Mr. Edwards was conducting a church meeting. A report of the purpose got abroad, and many persons came to the meeting, upon which it was thought most proper that the church business should be laid aside, and that Mr. Edwards should go into the pulpit. This he did, and after singing and prayer the prisoners came in with their shackles and fetters on. Mr. Edwards, in describing the scene, says:

'Many were moved at the sight. As for myself, I was obliged for some time to stop to give vent to tears. When I recovered I gave out part of a hymn suitable to the occasion, then prayed. The subject of discourse was, "This is a faithful saying," and the poor prisoners shed abundance of tears while I was explaining the several parts of the text, and especially when I turned and addressed myself immediately to them. The house was thronged, and I suppose not a dry eye in the whole place—nothing but weeping and sorrow; and the floods of tears which gushed from the eyes of the two prisoners were very melting.'

The good man continues: 'When we had concluded I went and spoke some encouraging words p. 247by way of supporting them under their sorrow. They then desired I should see them in the evening, which I did, and called upon Mr. Blindle on the way; the old gentleman went along with me to the prison, and was one who prayed with them with much fervour and enlargement of heart. We spent nearly two hours with them, and a crowd of people were present.' On another occasion we find an American Indian preaching in the pulpit—a novelty in 1767. He came over with a Dr. Whitaker, of Norwich, in America, to collect money for the education and conversion of Indians, and at Tackard Street the people raised the very respectable sum of #80 for the purpose. In 1561 Queen Elizabeth paid Ipswich a visit. At that time the place was a little too

Protestant for her. Strype writes: 'Here Her Majesty took a great dislike to the impudent behaviour of most of the ministers and readers, there being many weak ones among them, and little or no order observed in the public service, and few or none wearing the surplice, and the Bishop of Norwich was thought remiss, and that he winked at schismatics. But more particularly she was offended with the clergy's marriage, and that in cathedrals and colleges there were so many wives and children and widows seen, p. 248which, she said, was contrary to the intent of the founders, and so much tending to the interruption of the studies of those who were placed there. Therefore she issued an order to all dignitaries, dated August 9, at Ipswich, to forbid all women to the lodgings of cathedrals or colleges, and that upon pain of losing their ecclesiastical promotion.' From this it is clear that when Elizabeth was Queen there was little chance of the Women's Rights Question finding a favourable hearing. The Queen was succeeded by monarchs after her own heart. In 1636 Prynne published his 'Newes from Ipswich,' 'discovering certain late detestable practices of some domineering Lordly Prelates to undermine the established doctrine and discipline of our Church, extirpate all orthodox sincere preachers and preaching of God's Word, usher in popery, idolatry and superstition.' For this publication Prynne was sentenced to be fined #5,000 to the King, to lose the remainder of his ears, to be branded on both cheeks, and to be perpetually imprisoned in Carnarvon Castle. At that time the Ipswich people were far too Liberal for the powers existing. Ipswich news nowadays is little calculated to displease anyone, and governments and kings are less prone to take p. 249offence at the exercise of free thought and free speech.

Ipswich people make their way. Miss Reeve—who wrote the 'Old English Baron,' a popular tale years ago—was the daughter of the Rev. William Reeve of St. Nicholas Church. Another Ipswich lady, Mrs. Keeley, who lives on in her grand old age, was certainly one of the most popular performers of her day.

Two hundred years ago, no city man was better known than Thomas Firmin, who was born at Ipswich, described in his biography as 'a very large and populous town in the county of Suffolk,' in 1632. He was of Puritan parentage, and bound apprentice in the city of London, and then began business as a linen-draper on the modest capital of #100. In a little while he married and was enabled to dispense a generous hospitality, seeking all opportunities of becoming acquainted with persons of worth, whether foreigners or his fellow-countrymen. Amongst his special friends were Wilkins, Bishop of Chester, and Archbishop Tillotson, at that time the afternoon lecturer at St. Lawrence's. During the time of the plague he managed to secure work for the London poor, and after the fire he erected a warehouse on the banks of the p. 250Thames, where coal and corn were sold at cost price. In 1676 he built a great factory in Little Britain, for the employment of the needy and industrious in the linen manufacture; he also relieved poor debtors in prison. The great work of his later years was in connection with the Blue Coat School. He was also one of the Governors of St. Thomas's Hospital, which he did much to rescue from the wretched condition in which he found it. When the French refugees, in consequence of the revocation of the Edict of Nantes, were driven over to this country, Firmin exerted himself powerfully on their behalf, and sent some of them to Ipswich to engage in manufacturing there. He also had a good deal to do with Ireland, when, as now, the country was torn by contending factions. At a large expense he also educated many boys and set them up in trade. He was also one of the first of the avowed and ardent friends and advocates of a free thought, of which there were few supporters in England at that day—even among the countrymen of Milton and John Locke. Unitarians were rare in the days when Firmin proclaimed himself one. Altogether he was one of the best men of his age, and well deserved to be buried in Christchurch, Newgate, among the Bluecoat p. 251School boys, to whom he had ever been such a friend, and to have the memorial pillar erected in his honour by Lady Clayton in Marden Park, Surrey. It is to be hoped that the memorial remains, though, alas! the noble mansion at one time inhabited by Wilberforce, and where the great philanthropist's celebrated son, the Bishop of Oxford was born, and where I have spent more than one pleasant day when Sir John Puleston lived there, has been since burnt down.

p. 252CHAPTER IX.
an old-fashioned town.

Woodbridge and the country round—Bernard Barton—Dr. Lankester—An old Noncon.

The traveller as he leaves the English coast for Antwerp or Rotterdam or the northern ports of Germany, may remember that the last glimpse of his native land is the light from Orford Ness, which is a guiding star to the mariner as he ploughs his weary way along the deep. Of that part of Suffolk little is known to the community at large. When I was a boy it was looked upon as an *ultima Thule*, where the people were in a primitive state of civilization; where shops and towns and newspapers and good roads were unknown; where traditions of smuggling yet remained. Few ever went into that region, and those who did, when they returned, did not bring back with them encouraging reports. Barren sandy moors, along which the bitter east wind perpetually blew, fatal p. 253alike to vegetation and human life, were the chief characteristics of a district the natives of which were not rich, at any rate as regards this world's goods. Orford, like Dunwich, was once a place of some importance. 'A large and populous town with a castle of reddish stone,' writes Camden, but in his time a victim of the sea's ingratitude; 'which withdraws itself little by little, and begins to envy it the advantages of a harbour.' In the time of Henry I., writes Ralph de Coggeshall, when Bartholomew de Glanville was Governor of its castle, some fishermen there caught a wild man in their nets. 'All the parts of his body resembled those of a man. He had hair on his head, a long-peaked beard, and about the breast was exceeding hairy and rough. But at length he made his escape into the sea, and was never seen more,' which was a pity, as undoubtedly he was the 'missing link.' Besides, as Camden remarks, the fact was a confirmation of what the common people of his time remarked. 'Whatever is produced in any part of nature is in the sea,' and shows 'that not all is fabulous what Pliny has written about the Triton on the coasts of Portugal, and the sea man in the Straits of Gibraltar.' Nor is that the only wonder connected with the district. Close by is p.

254Aldborough, where the poet Crabbe learned to become, as Byron calls him,

'Nature's sternest painter, but the best;'

and as Camden writes, 'Hard by, when in the year 1555 all the corn throughout England was choakt in the ear by unseasonable weather, the inhabitants tell you that in the beginning of autumn there grew peas miraculously among the rocks, and that they relieved the dearth in those parts. But the more thinking people affirm that pulse cast upon the shore by shipwreck used to grow there now and then, and so quite exclude the miracle.' At the present the crag-beds are the most interesting feature to the visitor, especially if he be of a geological turn. These are so rich in fossil shells that you may find some of the latter in almost every house in Ipswich. The Coralline Crag is the oldest bed; but this formation does not occur in an undisturbed state, except in Sudbourne Park and about Orford. A drive thither from Ipswich, through Woodbridge, conveys the traveller through some of the loveliest scenery in Suffolk, and the numerous exposures of Coralline Crag in Sudbourne Park, which is about two miles from Orford, will amply repay the traveller, on account of the number of fossils which he can there obtain, and the ease p. 255with which he can extract them. In this neighbourhood live the far-famed Garrett family, one of whom, as Mrs. Dr. Anderson, is well known in London society, as is also her sister, Mrs. Fawcett, the wife of the late popular M.P. for Hackney. Close by is Leiston Abbey, originally one of Black Canons, consisting of several subterranean chapels, various offices and a church, which appears to have been a handsome structure, faced with flint and freestone. The interior was plain and undecorated, yet massive. A large extent of the neighbouring fields was enclosed with walls, which have been demolished, as was to be expected, for the sake of the materials. We hear much of the dead cities of the Zuyder Zee. On her eastern coast England has her dead cities. Dunwich, of which I have already spoken, is one. Orford, now known solely by its lighthouse, is another; Blythburgh, in the church of which is the tomb of Anna, King of the East Angles, who was slain in 654, is a third. Like Tyre and Sidon, these places had their merchant princes, who lived delicately, and whose ships traded far and near. It is said incorrectly of Love, that it

'At sight of human ties
Spreads its soft wings and in a moment flies.'

The remark is truer of commerce, which is a law to p. 256itself, and which defies Acts of Parliament and royal patronage. Hence it is the east coast of Suffolk is so rich in melancholy remains of ancient cities, now given over to decay. In my young days the chief town of this district was Woodbridge. Manufactories were then unknown. The steam-engine had not then been utilized for the everyday use of man, and farmers, peasants, coal and corn merchants, solely inhabited the district, and in Woodbridge especially the latter rose and flourished for a time.

How it was, I know not, but nevertheless such was the fact, that the Ipswich of my youthful days seemed to have little, if any, literary associations connected with it. The celebrated Mr. Fulcher published his 'Ladies' Pocket-book' at Sudbury, which had a great reputation in its day, and for which very distinguished people used to write. It was, in fact, more of an annual than a pocket-book, and was patronized accordingly. Then there was James Bird, living at Yoxford, 'the garden of Suffolk,' as it was called. Woodbridge had a still higher reputation. James Bird kept a shop, and was supposed to be a Unitarian; but Bernard Barton was in a bank, and, besides, he was a Quaker, and Quakers all the world over are, p. 257or were, famous for their goodness and their wealth. The fame of the Quaker-poet conferred quite a literary reputation on the district, and the more so as no one at that time associated Quakerism with literary faculty in any way. Now and then, it is true, the Stricklands talked of a charming young Quaker, who indeed once or twice called at our house to see Susanna when she was staying there; but Allan Ransome—for it is to him I refer—did not pursue literature or poetry to any great extent, and instead preferred to develop the manufacture of agricultural implements—a manufacture which, carried on under the same name, is now one of the chief industries of the busy and thriving town of Ipswich, and employs quite a thousand men. Woodbridge then bore away the palm from the county capital, as the home of literature and poetry and romance. As a town, it is more prettily situated than are most East Anglian villages and towns. The principal thoroughfare, as you rode through it by one of the Yarmouth coaches, that connected it at that time with the Metropolis, was long and narrow. If you turned off to the right you came to the Market-place, where were the leading shops. On your left you reached the Quay and the river, where a few coasters were employed, chiefly in the p. 258coal and corn trade. In our time Woodbridge has done its duty to the State. Dr. Edwin Lankester the well-known coroner for Middlesex, came from Melton, close by, the High Street of which gradually terminates in the Woodbridge thoroughfare; and the lately deceased Lord Hatherley, one of England's most celebrated lawyers, was educated in that district, and took his wife from the same happy land. The body of the late Lord Hatherley, the great Whig Lord Chancellor, we were told the other day, was interred in the family vault of Great Bearings, Suffolk. His mother was a Woodbridge lady, a Miss Page. Lord Hatherley's father was the far-famed Liberal Alderman, Sir Matthew Wood, for many years M.P. for the City of London, and Queen Caroline's trusted friend and counsellor. Lord Hatherley married, in 1830, Charlotte, the only daughter of the late Major Edward Moore, of Great Bealings, Suffolk, but was left a widower in 1878. He devoted much time to religious work, so long as he had the strength to undertake it. He was the author of a work entitled 'The Continuity of Scripture, as declared by the Testimony of Our Lord and the Evangelists and the Apostles', which has passed through three or four editions. He was created an Hon. D.C.L. of Oxford in 1851, p. 259was an Hon. Student of Christ Church, Oxford, a Governor of the Charterhouse, and a member of the Fishmongers' Company, of which his father had at one time been Prime Warden. Major Moore himself was a great authority on Suffolk literature and antiquities, and published more than one book—now very scarce—on the interesting theme.

As to Dr. Lankester, all Woodbridge was scandalized when it was announced that he was articled to a medical man. 'What, make a doctor of him!' said the local gossips at the time. 'They had much better make a butcher of him.' And not a little were the good people astonished when he came to town, and was signally successful as a medical lecturer, and as an advocate of the sanitary principles which in our day have come to be recognised as essential to the welfare of the State. Dr. Lankester was in great request as a writer on medical subjects in a popular manner, and did undoubtedly much good in his day. A good many genteel people lived in the neighbourhood of Woodbridge, and it had a society to which it can lay no claim at the present time. Edward Fitzgerald, the friend of Thackeray and Carlyle, himself an author of no mean repute, lived close by.

That genteel people should have pitched their p. 260tents in or around Woodbridge is not much to be wondered at, as the neighbourhood was certainly attractive and convenient at the same time. The scenery around is as interesting as any that could be found, at any rate, in that part of England. The drive from Tuddenham to Woodbridge, says Mr. Taylor, in his 'Ipswich Handbook,' is perhaps unequalled in Suffolk. On the road you pass through the villages of Little and Great Bealings, and if you are on the look-out for spots which an artist would love to study, you may make a very short detour to Playford. The churches, both of Little and of Great Bealings, are very ancient, and well deserve a visit; but the Woodbridge Road itself passes through some very pretty scenery. Rushmere Heath, in the early summer time, when the gorse is in bloom, is one mass of yellow, in the cleared spaces of which may usually be seen a gipsy encampment. The gibbet once stood on this heath, and in former times it seems to have been the place where executions usually took place. It was here that in 1783 a woman, named Bedingfield, was burnt for murdering her husband. In the early part of this century, when there were many alarms as to a French invasion, and it was the firm belief of the old ladies that one fine morning p. 261Bony would land upon our shores, and carry them all away captive, many were the reviews of soldiers held there by the Duke of Cambridge — whose house has been pointed out to me at Woodbridge — and the Duke of Kent. At that time it was the fashion to exercise the volunteers on a Sunday, a practice which would not be sanctioned in our more religious age. It is a beautiful ride through Kesgrave. Dense plantations abound on both sides, and in May the chorus of nightingales is described as something wonderful. In the word 'Kesgrave' we have an allusion to the barrows or tumuli to be seen on Kesgrave Heath. There are several of these erections remaining to this day, and perhaps tradition is warranted in speaking of the spot as the site whereon the Danes and Saxons met in deadly fight. It is certain that the former frequently came up the Deben and the Orwell. At Martlesham you see a creek, richly wooded on both sides, which flows up from the River Deben. It is a striking object at high water, but by no means so striking as the sign of the village public-house—the head of a huge wooden lion painted with the brightest of reds. It was originally the figure-head of a Dutch man-of-war, one of the fleet defeated at the famous battle of Sole Bay. Be p. 262that as it may, no sign is better known than that of Martlesham Red Lion. 'As red as Martlesham Lion' is still a common figure of speech throughout East Suffolk, and I am glad to see that in the beautiful East Anglian etchings of Mr. Edwards, a Suffolk lawyer, who turned artist, Martlesham Red Lion has justice done to it at last.

Woodbridge, which the guide-book in 1844 described as a thriving town and port—I question whether it is thriving now—is situated on the western bank of the Deben, about nine miles above the mouth of the river, and about eight miles to the north of Ipswich. In Domesday Book the place is called Udebridge, of which its present name is no doubt a corruption. Mr. William White, whom I have already quoted, says: 'Fifty years ago only one daily coach and a weekly waggon passed through the town to and from London; but more than twelve conveyances (coaches, omnibuses and carriers' waggons) now pass daily between the hours of six in the morning and twelve at noon, and persons may travel from Woodbridge to London in a few hours for ten shillings, instead of paying three times that amount, and being thirteen hours on the road, as was formerly the case.' The railway has now rendered p. 263it possible for people to travel at a quicker speed and at a cheaper rate. In London we have a Woodbridge Street, in the neighbourhood of Clerkenwell Green, which points to a connection between the poorer part of the City and the picturesque Suffolk town on the banks of the Deben, and this gives me occasion to speak of Thomas Seckford, Esq., one of the masters of the Court of Requests, and Surveyor of the Court of Wards and Liveries in the reign of Queen Elizabeth. He was not less distinguished in the profession of the law than in the other polite accomplishments of the age in which he lived, and to his patronage of his servant, Christopher Saxton, the public were indebted for the first set of county maps, which were engraved by his encouragement and at his request. He represented Ipswich in three Parliaments, and died without issue in 1588, aged seventy-two. In Woodbridge his name is perpetuated by a handsome pile of buildings known as the Seckford Almshouses and Schools, to which the property in Clerkenwell is devoted. At the time of his decease that property produced about #112 a year; in 1768 it was said to be of the yearly value of #563. In 1826 an Act of Parliament was obtained to enable the governors of the almshouses to grant building and p. 264other leases, to take down many of the old buildings, to erect new premises, and repair and alter old ones, and to lay out new streets on the charity estate in Clerkenwell, and, in consequence, we find in 1830 the estate producing a rental of more than #3,000 a year. In 1844 the yearly rental had risen to #4,000. Since then it has much increased, and all this is devoted to the benefit of the Woodbridge poor.

In 1806 Bernard Barton, the Quaker poet, came to live at Woodbridge. When fourteen years old he was apprenticed to Mr. Samuel Jessup, a shopkeeper in Halstead, Essex. 'There I stood,' he writes, 'for eight years behind the counter of the corner shop at the top of Halstead Hill, kept to this day (November 9, 1828) by my old master and still worthy uncle, S. Jessup.' In Woodbridge he married a niece of his old master, and went into partnership with her brother as corn and coal merchant. But she died in giving birth to the Lucy Barton whose name still, unless I am mistaken, adorns our literature. Bernard gave up business and retired into the bank of the Messrs. Alexander, where he continued for forty years, working within two days of his death. He had always been fond of books, and was one of the p. 265most active members of a Woodbridge Book Club, and had been in the habit of writing and sending to his friends occasional copies of verse. In 1812 he published his first volume, called 'Metrical Effusions,' and began a correspondence with Southey. A complimentary copy of verses which he had addressed to the author of the 'Queen's Wake,' just then come into notice, brought him long and vehement letters from the Ettrick—letters full of thanks to Barton and praises of himself, and a tragedy 'that will astonish the world ten times more than the "Queen's Wake,"' to which justice could not be done in Edinburgh, and which Bernard Barton was to try to get represented in London. In 1825 one of Bernard's volumes of poems had run into a fifth edition, and of another George IV. had accepted the dedication. Thus prompted to exertion, he worked too hard; banking all day and writing poetry all night were too much for him. Lamb, however, cheered up the dyspeptic poet. 'You are too much apprehensive about your complaint,' he wrote. 'I know many that are always writing of it and live on to a good old age. I knew a merry fellow — you partly know him, too — who, when his medical adviser told him he had drunk all *that part*, congratulated p. 266himself, now his liver was gone, that he should be the longest liver of the two.' Southey wrote in a soberer vein. 'My friend, go to bed early; and if you eat suppers, read afterwards, but never compose, that you may lie down with a quiet intellect. There is an intellectual as well as a religious peace of mind, and without the former be assured there can be no health for a poet.'

At times Bernard Barton seems to have been troubled about money matters. On one occasion he appears to have made up his mind to have done with banking and devote himself to literature. 'Keep to your bank,' wrote Lamb, 'and the bank will keep you. Trust not to the public: you may hang, starve, drown yourself, for anything that worthy personage cares. I bless every star that Providence, not seeing good to make me independent, has seen it next good to settle me on the stable foundation of Leadenhall. Sit down, good B. B., in the banking office. What! is there not from six to eleven p.m. six days in the week? and is there not all Sunday?' Fortunately for B. B., friends came to his rescue. A few members of his Society, including some of the wealthier of his own family, raised among them #1,200 for his benefit. The scheme originated with Joseph John Gurney, p. 267of Norwich, and in 1824 when the money was collected, it was felt that #1,200 was a great deal for a poet to receive. Bernard Barton's daughter married a Suffolk gentleman, well-to-do in the world, but the lady and gentleman had not congenial minds, and parted almost as soon as the honeymoon was over.

B. B. was a great correspondent. As a banker's clerk, necessarily his journeys were few and far between. Once or twice he visited Charles Lamb. He once also met Southey at Thomas Clarkson's, at Playford Hall, perhaps the most picturesque old house in East Anglia, where the latter resided, and of which I have a distinct recollection, as, on the terrace before the moat with which it was surrounded, I once saw the venerable philanthropist and his grandchildren. Now and then B. B. also visited the Rev. Mr. Mitford at Benhall, a village between Woodbridge and Saxmundham, who was then engaged in editing the Aldine edition of the English Poets. But B. B.'s correspondents were numerous. Poor, unfortunate L. E. L. sent him girlish letters. Mrs. Hemans was also a correspondent, as were the Howitts and Mrs. Opie and Dr. Drake, of Hadley, whose literary disquisitions are now, alas! forgotten; and poor Charles Lloyd, p. 268whose father wrote of his son's many books 'that it is easier to write them than to gain numerous readers.' Dr. Bowring and Josiah Conder were also on writing terms with the Quaker poet. His excursions, his daughter tells us, rarely extended beyond a few miles round Woodbridge, to the vale of Dedham, Constable's birthplace and painting-room; or to the neighbouring seacoast, including Aldborough, doubly dear to him from its association with the memory and poetry of Crabbe. Once upon a time he dined with Sir Robert Peel, when he had the pleasure of meeting Airy, the late Astronomer Royal, whom he had known as a lad at Playford. The dinner with Sir Robert Peel ended satisfactorily, as it resulted in the bestowal by the Queen on the poet of a pension of #100 a year. He was now beyond the fear of being tempted to commit forgery, and being hung in consequence — a possibility, which was the occasion of one of Lamb's wittiest letters. The gentle Elia made merry over the chance of a Quaker poet being hung.

Amiable and liberal as was Bernard Barton, he could and did strike hard when occasion required. In East Anglia, when I was a lad, there was a great deal of intolerance — almost as much as exists in society circles at the present day — and p. 269that is saying a great deal. Churchmen, in their ignorance, were ready to put down Dissent in every way, and occasionally, by their absurdity, they roused the righteous ire of the Quaker poet. One of them, for instance, had said at a public meeting: 'This was the opinion he had formed of Dissenters, that they were wolves in sheep's clothing.' Whereupon B. B. wrote:

> 'Wolves in sheep's clothing! bitter words and big;
> But who applies them? first the speaker scan;
> A suckling Tory! an apostate Whig!
> Indeed a very silly, weak young man!

'What such an one may either think or say,
With sober people matters not one pin;
In *their* opinion his own senseless bray
Proves *him* the ass wrapt in a lion's skin!'

Better is the following address to a certain Dr. E.:

'A bullying, brawling, champion of the Church,
Vain as a parrot screaming on her perch;
And like that parrot screaming out by rote,
The same stale, flat, unprofitable note;
Still interrupting all debate
With one eternal cry of "Church and State!"
With all the High Tory's ignorance increased,
By all the arrogance that makes the priest;
One who declares upon his solemn word
The Voluntary system is absurd;
He well may say so, for 'twere hard to tell
Who would support him did not law compel.'

p. 270A prophet, it is said, is not honoured in his own country. Bernard Barton was happily the rare exception that proves the rule. I remember being at the launching of a vessel, bought and owned by a Woodbridge man, called the *Bernard Barton*; it was the first time I had ever seen a ship launched, and I was interested accordingly. The ultimate fate of the craft is unknown to history. On one occasion she was reported in the shipping list amongst the arrivals at some far-off port as the *Barney Burton*. Such is fame!

Of his local reputation Bernard was not a little proud. His little town was vain of him. It was something to go into the bank and get a cheque cashed by the poet. The other evening I went to the house of a Woodbridge man who has done well in London, and lives in one of the few grand old houses which yet adorn Stoke Newington Green—just a stone's throw from where Samuel Rogers dwelt—and there in the drawing-room were Bernard Barton's own chair and cabinet preserved with as much pious care as if he had been a Shakespeare or a Milton. Bernard Barton made no secret of his vocation, and when the time had come that he had delivered himself of a new poem, it was his habit to call on one or other of his friends and

p. 271discuss the matter over a bottle of port—port befitting the occasion; no modern liquor of that name—

'Not such as that
You set before chance comers,
But such whose father grape grew fat
On Lusitanian summers.'

And then there was a good deal of talk, as was to be expected, on things in general, for B. B. loved his joke and was full of anecdote— anecdote, perhaps, not always of the most refined character. But what could you expect at such happy times from a man brimful of human nature, who had to pose all life under the double weight of decorum imposed on him, in the first place as a Quaker, and in the second place as a banker's clerk?

Bernard Barton, as I recollect him, was somewhat of a dear old man—short in person, red in face, with dark brown hair. He was, as I have said, a clerk in a bank, but his poetry had elevated him, somehow, to the rank of a provincial lion, and at certain houses, where the dinner was good and the wine was ditto, he ever was a welcome guest. I dined with him at the house of a friend in Woodbridge, and it seemed to me that he cared more for good feeding and a glass of wine and a p. 272pinch of snuff than the sacred Nine. Of course at that time I had not been educated up to the fitting state of mind with which the philosopher of our day proceeds to the performance of the mysteries of dinner. Dining had at that time not been elevated to the rank of a science, to the study of which the most acute intellects devote their highest energies; nor had flowers then been invoked to lend an additional grace to the dining-table. Besides, dinners such as Mr. Black gives at Brighton, scientific dinners, such as those feasts with which Sir Henry Thompson regales his friends, were unknown. Nevertheless, now and then we managed to dine comfortably off roast beef or lamb, a slice of boiled or roast fowl, a bit of plum-pudding or fruit tart, a crust of bread and cheese, with—tell it not in Gath, publish it not in the streets of Askalon—sherry and Madeira at dinner, and a few glasses of fine old fruity port after. Some Shakespearian quotations—unknown to me then, for Shakespeare was little quoted in purely evangelical circles, either in Church or Dissent—a reference to Sir Walter Scott's earlier

German translations, formed about the sum and substance of the conversation which took place between the poet and my host; all the rest was p. 273principally social gossip and an exchange of pleasantries between the poet and his friend, whom he addressed familiarly as 'mine ancient.' It was a great treat to me, of course, to dine with Bernard Barton, the Quaker poet. Once upon a time a Quaker minister had come to Woodbridge on a preaching tour, and all the Quakers, male and female, small and great, rich and poor, were ranged before him. When Bernard Barton was announced, the good old man said, 'Barton—Barton—that's a name I don't recollect.' The bearer of the name replied it would be strange if he did, seeing that they had never met before. Suddenly looking up, the minister exclaimed, 'Art thou the versifying man?' Unlike the venerable stranger, I had no need to ask the question, as in my mother's album there was more than one letter from the genial B. B.

I can well recall the room in which I dined with the poet. My host had come into a handsome fortune by marrying a wealthy widow—one of the possibilities of a Dissenting minister's situation—and he had retired from the ministry to cultivate literature and literary men. As I think of that room and that dinner, I am reminded of the wonderful contrast effected within the last age. p. 274At that time the dinner-table presented a far less picturesque appearance than it does now. We had always pudding before meat; the latter was solid, and in the shape of a joint. Nor was it handed round by servants, but carved by the host or his lady. Silver forks were unknown, and electro-plate had not then been invented. Vegetables, also, were deficient as regards quantity and quality compared with the supply at a respectable dinner nowadays. In manners the change is equally remarkable. It was said of a nobleman, a personal friend of George III., and a model gentleman of his day, that he had made the tour of Europe without ever touching the back of his travelling carriage. That includes an idea of self-denial utterly unknown to all the young people of to-day. The study now is how to make our houses more comfortable, and to furnish them most luxuriously. Then, perhaps, there was but one sofa in the house, and that was repellent rather than attractive. Easy-chairs were few and far between. Lounging of any kind was out of the question. In the drawing-room, the furniture was of the same uncomfortable description, and there were none of the modern appliances which exist to make ladies and gentlemen happy. Couches, p. 275antimacassars, photographs, were unknown. One picture invariably to be seen was a painting of a favourite steed, with the owner looking at it in a state of intense admiration; and a few family portraits might be ostentatiously displayed. As to pianos, there never was but one in the house; and a billiard-table would have been considered as the last refuge of human depravity. In sitting-rooms and bedrooms and passages there was a great deficiency of carpets and of oilcloth. But furniture was furniture then, and could stand a good deal of wear and tear; while as to the spare bed in the best room, with its enormous four posts and its gigantic funereal canopy and its heavy curtains, through which no breath of fresh air could penetrate, all I can say is that people slept in it and survived the operation—so wonderfully does nature adapt itself to circumstances the most adverse.

This reference to Bernard Barton reminds me of a portrait he has left in one of his pleasant letters of a Suffolk yeoman, a class of whose virtues I can testify from personal experience. 'He was a hearty old yeoman of eighty-six, and had occupied the farm in which he lived and died about fifty-five years. Social, hospitable, friendly, a liberal master to his labourers, a kind neighbour, and a right merry p. 276companion within the limits of becoming mirth. In politics a stanch Whig, in his theological creed as sturdy a Dissenter; yet with no more party spirit in him than a child. He and I belonged to the same book-club for about forty years. . . . Not that he greatly cared about books or was deeply read in them, but he loved to meet his neighbours and get them round him on any occasion or no occasion at all. As a fine specimen of the true English yeoman, I have met with few to equal, if any to surpass him, and he looked the character as well as he acted it, till within a few years, when the strong man was bowed by bodily infirmity. About twenty-six years ago, in his dress costume of a blue coat and yellow buckskins, a finer sample of John Bullism you would rarely see. It was the whole study of his long life to make the few who revolved round him in his little orbit as happy as he seemed to be himself. Yet I was gravely queried when I happened to say that his children had asked me to write a few lines to his memory, whether I could do this in keeping with the general tone of my poetry—the speaker doubted if he was a decidedly pious character! He had at times in his altitude been known to vociferate a song, of which the chorus was certainly not teetotalism:

> p. 277'"Sing old Rose, and burn the bellows,
> Drink and drive dull care away."'

Bernard Barton goes on to describe the deceased yeoman as a diligent attendant at the meeting-house, a frequent and serious reader of the Bible, and the head of an orderly and well-regulated house. He is described as knowing Dr. Watts' hymns almost by heart, and as singing them on Sunday at meeting with equal fervour and unction. Bernard Barton feared in 1847—the date of his epistle—the breed of such men was dying out. It is to be feared in East Anglia the race is quite extinct. In our meeting-house at Wrentham, when I was a lad, there were several such. I am afraid there is not one there now. The sons and daughters have left the old rustic houses, and gone out into the world. They have become respectable, and go to church, and have lost a good deal of the vigour and independence of their forefathers. In all the East Anglian meeting-houses fifty years ago such men abounded. Of a Sunday, with their blue coats and kerseymere knee-breeches, and jolly red laces, they looked more like country squires than common farmers. They drove up to the meeting-house yard with very superior gigs and cattle. In their houses creature comforts of all known kinds p. 278were to be found. Tea—a hearty meal, not of mere bread-and-butter, but of ham and cake as well—was served up in the parlour, with a glass or two of real home-brewed ale, amber-coloured, of a quality now unknown, and which was wonderfully refreshing after a long walk or drive. Then, if it were summer, there was a stroll in the big garden, well planted with fruit-trees and strawberry-beds, and adorned with flowers—old-fashioned, perhaps, but rich, nevertheless, in colour and perfume. In one corner there was sure to be an arbour, all covered with honeysuckle, such as Izaak Walton himself would have approved; and there, while the seniors over their long pipes discussed politics and theology, and corn and cattle, the younger ones would make their first feeble efforts, all unconsciously, perhaps, to conjugate the verb 'to love.' Outside the church organizations these old yeomen lived and died. There was a flavour of the world about them. They would dine at market ordinaries, and perhaps would stop an hour in the long room of the public-house, where they put up their horses, to smoke a pipe and take a drop of brandy-and-water for the good of the landlord. Now and then—sometimes to the sorrow of their wives, who were often church-members—they would join, as I have indicated, in p. 279a song of an objectionable character when severely criticised. Perhaps their parson would be much exercised on their behalf; but surely the noble spirit of humanity in these old yeomen, at any rate, was as worthy of admiration as the Puritanic faith of the past—or as the honest doubt of the present age. If I mistake not, the fine old yeoman to whom Bernard Barton referred lived not far from Seckford Hall.

Woodbridge has some claim to consideration from the Nonconformist point of view. In 1648 a schoolmistress, Elizabeth Warren, published a pamphlet, 'The Old and Good Way Vindicated, in a Treatise, wherein Divers Errours, both in Judgment and Practice incident to these Declining Days, are Unmasked for the Caution of humble Christians.' From the same town also there issued 'The Preacher Sent: a Vindication of the Liberty of Public Preaching by Some Men not Ordained.' The author of this book, or one of the authors of it, was the Rev. Frederick Woodall, the first pastor of the Free Church—'a man of learning, ability, and piety, a strict Independent, zealous for the fifth monarchy, and a considerable sufferer after his ejectment.' He had, we are told, to contend with a tedious embarrassment, through the persecuting p. 280spirit that for many years prevailed, and considerably cramped the success of his ministry. Woodbridge is one of the churches which Mr. Harmer refers to in his 'Miscellaneous Works,' as being rigidly Congregationalist, and which conducted its affairs rather according to the heads of Savoy Confession than the heads of Agreement. When I was a boy the pastor was a Mr. Pinchback, who seems to have been a worthy successor of godly men, equally attractive and successful. He had previously settled at Ware. It is recorded of the good divine that on one occasion he had to leave his wife at the point of death, as it seemed, to go to chapel. In the course of the service he mentioned the fact of her illness, and announced in consequence that he would preach her funeral sermon on the following Sunday. But when the following Sunday came the lady was better, and lived for many years to assist her husband in his godly work. In the rural districts the Baptists flourished immensely.

At Grundisburgh there preached for many years to a large congregation a worthy man of the name of Collins, who was one of the leading lights of the body which rejoiced in a John Foreman and a Brother Wells. People who live in London cannot p. 281have forgotten Jemmy Wells, of the Surrey Tabernacle, and his grotesque and telling anecdotes. One can scarcely imagine how people could ever believe the things Wells used to say as to the Lord's dealings with him; but they did, and his funeral — in South London, at any rate — was almost as numerously attended as that of Arthur, Duke of Wellington. I expect high-and-dry Baptists have been not a little troublesome in their day, and in East Anglia they were more numerous than in London. It may be that they have helped to weaken Dissent in that part of the world. Men of independent intellect must have been not a little shocked by that unctuous familiarity with God and the devil which is the characteristic of that class. On a Sunday morning Jemmy Wells, as his admirers called him, would describe in the most graphic manner what the devil had said to him in the course of the week; and on one memorable occasion, at any rate, described with much force the shame he felt at having to tell the gentleman in black that his people's memories, unfortunately, were somewhat remiss in the matter of pew-rents. Brother Collins avoided such flights, but he was an attractive preacher to all the country round, nevertheless. Truly such a one was needed in that p. 282district. At Rendham, a village near Saxmundham, lived a godly minister of the Church of England. In 1844, speaking to a friend of the writer, he said that when he came into the county, between thirty and forty years before, there was only one other clergyman and himself between Ipswich and Great Yarmouth who preached the Gospel, and that sometimes the squire of the parish would hold up his watch to him to bid him close his sermon. In some places where he went to preach he had to have a body-guard to prevent his being mobbed and pelted with rotten eggs on account of his evangelical principles.

p. 283CHAPTER X.
milton's suffolk schoolmaster.

Stowmarket—The Rev. Thomas Young—Bishop Hall and the Smectymnian divines—Milton's mulberry-tree—Suffolk relationships.

'My father destined me,' writes John Milton, in his 'Defensio Secunda,' 'while yet a little boy, for the study of humane letters, which I served with such eagerness that, from the twelfth year of my age, I scarcely ever went from my lessons to bed before midnight, which, indeed, was the first cause of injury to my eyes, to whose natural weakness there were also added frequent headaches; all which not retarding my natural impetuosity in learning, he caused me to be instructed both at the Grammar School and under other masters at home.' Of the latter, the best known was the Rev. Thomas Young, the Puritan minister, of Stowmarket, Suffolk.

It is generally claimed for Young that he was p. 284an East Anglian. Professor Masson has, however, settled the question that he was a Scotchman, of the University of Aberdeen. Be that as it may, like most Scotchmen, he made his way to England, and was employed by Mr. Milton, the scrivener of Bread Street, to teach his gifted son. As he seems to have been married at the time, it is not probable that he resided with his pupil, but only visited him daily. Never had master a better pupil, or one who rewarded him more richly by the splendour of his subsequent career. The poet, writing to him a few years after he ceased to be his pupil, speaks of 'the incredible and singular gratitude he owed him on account of the services he had done him,' and calls God to witness that he reverenced him as his father. In a Latin elegy, after implying that Young was dearer to him than Socrates to Alcibiades, or than the great Stagyrite to his generous pupil, Alexander, he goes on to say: 'First, under his guidance, I explored the recesses of the Muses, and beheld the sacred green spots of the cleft summit of Parnassus and quaffed the Pierian cups, and, Clio favouring me, thrice sprinkled my joyful mouth with Castalian wine;' from which it is clear that Young had done his duty to his pupil, and that the latter ever regarded p. 285him with an affection as beautiful as rare. Never did a Rugby lad write of Arnold as

Milton of Thomas Young. How long the latter's preceptorship lasted cannot be determined with precision. 'It certainly closed,' writes Professor Masson, in that truly awful biography of his, 'when Young left England at the age of thirty-five, and became pastor of the congregation of British merchants settled at Hamburg.'

As one of the leaders of the Presbyterian party, Dr. Thomas Young became Vicar of Stowmarket in due time. He was one of the Smectymnian divines. As it is not every schoolboy who knows what the term means, let me explain who they were. Two or three hundred years ago people were much more controversial than they are now, and very fierce was the battle on the subject of the relative claims, from a Scriptural point of view, of Prelacy or Presbytery. One of the most distinguished champions of the former was Dr. Hall, Bishop of Norwich—a simple, godly, learned man, who deserves to be held in remembrance, if only for the way in which he got married. 'Being now settled,' he writes, 'in that sweet and civil county of Suffolk, the uncouth solitariness of my life, and the extreme incommodity of that single housekeeping, drew my p. 286thoughts, after two years, to condescend to the necessity of a married state, which God no less strangely provided for me; for walking from the church on Monday, in the Whitsun week, with a grave and reverend minister, I saw a comely and modest gentlewoman standing at the door of that house where we were invited to a wedding-dinner, and inquiring of that worthy friend whether he knew her, "Yes," quoth he, "I know her well, and have bespoken her for your wife." When I further demanded an account of that answer, he told me she was the daughter of a gentleman whom he much respected—Mr. George Whinniff, of Brettenham; that out of an opinion he had of the fitness of that match for me he had already treated with her father about it, whom he found very apt to entertain it. Advising me not to neglect the opportunity, and not concealing the just praises of the modesty, piety, good disposition, and other virtues that were lodged in that seemly presence, I listened to the motion as sent from God, and at last, upon due prosecution, happily prevailed, enjoying the comfortable society of that meethelp for the space of forty-nine years.' A young clergyman so good and amiable ought to have fared better as regards the days in which his lot was passed. Hall p. 287should have lived in some theological

Arcadia. As it was, he had to fight much and suffer much. In those distracted times he was all for peace. When the storm was brewing in Church and State, which for a time swept away Bishop and King, he published—but, alas! in vain—his 'Via Media.' 'I see,' he wrote, 'every man to rank himself unto a side, and to draw in the quarrel he affecteth. I see no man either holding or joining their hands for peace.' Bishop Hall was the most celebrated writer of his time in defence of the Church of England. Archbishop Laud got him to write on 'The Divine Right of Episcopacy,' nor could he have well placed the subject in abler hands. This was followed, after Laud had fallen, with 'An Humble Remonstrance to the High Court of Parliament,' in which treatise he vindicated the antiquity of liturgies and Episcopacy with admirable skill, meekness, and simplicity, yet with such strength of argument that five Presbyterian divines clubbed their wits together to frame an answer. These Presbyterian ministers were—Stephen Marshal, then lecturer at St. Margaret's, whom Baillie terms the best of the preachers in England; Edmund Calamy, who had long been a celebrated East Anglian preacher, first at Swaffham, then at Bury p. 288St. Edmunds, who, as we all know, refused a bishopric when offered him, and whom, therefore, at any rate, his adversaries must allow to have been sincere; Thomas Young, Matthew Newcomen, and William Spurstow. To this reply was given the name of Smectymnuus—a startling word, as Calamy calls it, made up of the initial letters of these names. This work, which was published in 1641, gave, says Dr. M'Crie, the first serious blow to Prelacy. It was composed in a style superior to that of the Puritans in general, and was, by the confession of the learned Bishop Wilkins, a capital work against Episcopacy. Dr. Kippis says, 'This piece is certainly written with great fierceness and asperity of language,' and quotes, as evidence, some strong things said against the practice of the prelates. But Neal, who has given a long account of the work, states that, if the rest of the clergy had been of the same temper and spirit with Bishop Hall, the controversy between him and the Smectymnian divines might have been compromised.

Stowmarket, as I have said, had the honour of being placed under the pastoral care of one of these Smectymnian divines. He came there in March, 1628, on the presentation of Mr. John p. 289Howe, a gentleman then residing in the town, and a man of wealth, whose ancestors had been great cloth-manufacturers in that place and neighbourhood. Since the time of Edward III. the cloth manufacture had been very active in Suffolk, and it is little to the credit of its merchants that we find them, in 1522, petitioning for the repeal of a royal law which inflicted a penalty against those who sold cloth which, when wetted, shrunk up, on the plea that, as such goods were made for a foreign market, the home-consumer was not injured. Stowmarket, when I was a lad, had reached its climax in a pecuniary sense. In the early part of the present century it was spoken of as a rising town. Situated as it was in the centre of the county, it was a convenient mart for barley, and great quantities of malt were made. Its other manufactures were sacking, ropes, and twine. Its tanneries were of a more recent date, as also its manufactory of gun-cotton, connected with which at one time there was an explosion of a most fatal and disastrous character. In 1763 it was connected with Ipswich by means of a canal, which was a great source of prosperity to the town. Up to the time of the great Reform Bill, it was the great place for county meetings, and for the nomination of the county representatives. In our p. 290day it has a population of 4,052. When I was a lad it was one of the first towns to welcome the Plymouth Brethren into Suffolk, and they are there still. The Independent Chapel for awhile suffered much from them. The pastor was a very worthy but somewhat dry preacher. His favourite quotation in the pulpit, when he would describe the attacks of the enemy of God and man, was

  'He worries whom he can't devour
  With a malicious joy.'

Suffolk had its great lawyers as well as Norfolk. The first to head the list is Ranulph de Glanville, a man of great parts, deep learning, for the times, eminent alike for his legal abilities and energetic mind. He was said, by one account, to have been born at Stowmarket. It is certain he founded Leiston Abbey, near Aldborough, and Bentley Priory. As Chief Justice under Henry II. he naturally was no favourite with Richard I., who deprived him of his office and made use of his wealth. He lived, however, to accompany Richard to the Holy Land, and died at the siege of Acre. His treatise on our laws is one of the earliest on record. It must be remembered also that Godwin, the author of 'Political Justice,' and 'Caleb Williams,' a novel still read — the husband of one gifted p. 291woman, and the father of another — was at one time an Independent minister at Stowmarket.

But to return to Dr. Young. He, like Mr. Newcomen, had become an East Anglian, and Smectymnuus may therefore more or less be said to have an East Anglian original. As the living of Stowmarket was at that time worth #300 a year, and as #300 a year then was quite equal to #600 a year now, Dr. Young must have been in comfortable circumstances while at Stowmarket. A likeness of him is hung up, or was preserved, in Stowmarket Vicarage. 'It,' wrote an old observer, 'possesses the solemn, faded yellowness of a man much given to austere meditation, yet there is sufficient energy in the eye and mouth to show, as he is preaching in Geneva gown and bands, that he is a man who could write and think, and speak with great vigour.' One of Milton's biographers terms him, contemptuously, a Puritan who cut his hair short. The Rev. Mr. Hollingsworth writes that it is an error to suppose that Young remained long as chaplain to merchants abroad. 'He must have remained generally in constant residence, because we possess his signature to the vestry accounts, in a curious quarto book, which contains the annual accounts of Stow upland Parish for eighty-four years. At the parish meetings, p. 292and at the audit of each year's accounts Vicar Young presided, with some exceptions, from the year 1629 to 1655, and his autograph is attached to each page.' As an author, Dr. Young had distinguished himself before he appeared as one of the Smectymnians. In 1639, while the Stuarts and the Bishops were doing all they could to break down the sanctity of the Sabbath, and to make it a day of vulgar revelry and rustic sport, Dr. Young published a thin quarto in Latin, entitled 'Dies Dominica,' containing a history of the institution of the Sabbath, and its vindication from all common and profane uses. There is no place of publication named, the signature is feigned, 'Theophilus Philo Kunaces Loncardiensis,' and in the copy reserved at Stowmarket is added, in characters by no means unlike that of the handwriting of the Vicar himself, 'Dr. Thos. Young, of Jesus.' The tractate is described as a very elaborate and learned compilation from the Fathers upon the sanctity of the Sabbath. A spirit of laborious and determined energy pervades it, nor is it unworthy the abilities and erudition of the author. The work was written at Stowmarket, and may have been published in

Ipswich. Its paper and type are coarse; the name of the author was concealed, because at that time p. 293a man who reverenced the Sabbath had a good chance of being brought before the Star Chamber, and of being roughly treated by Archbishop Laud, as an enemy to Church and State. About ten years before, Dr. Young had heard how, for writing his plea against Prelacy, Dr. Alexander Leighton had been cast into Newgate, dragged before the Star Chamber, where he was sentenced to have his ears cut off, to have his nose slit, to be branded in the face, to stand in the pillory, to be whipped at the post, to pay a fine of #10,000, and to suffer perpetual imprisonment. Dr. Young might well shrink from exposing himself to similar torture. But Dr. Young had other warnings, and much nearer home.

Dr. Young, like most of the men of that time, persecuted witches. These latter were supposed to have existed in great numbers, and a roving commission for their discovery was given to one Matthew Hopkins, of Manningtree, in Essex, to find them out in the eastern counties and execute the law upon them. It was a brutal business, and Hopkins followed it for three or four years. He proceeded from town to town and opened his courts. Stowmarket was one of the places he visited. The Puritans are said to have hung sixty p. 294witches in Suffolk, but the Puritans were not alone responsible. It is a fact that, up to fifty years ago two supposed witches lived in Stowmarket.

Dr. Young escaped the Star Chamber, but, like most good men who would be free at that time he had to fly his native land for awhile. Milton refers to this exile in his Latin elegy:

> 'Meantime alone
> Thou dwellest, and helpless on a soil unknown,
> Poor, and receiving from a foreign hand
> The aid denied thee in thy native land.'

It seems from this that the living at Stowmarket was under sequestration. A little while after Young is back in Stowmarket, and Milton thus describes his daily life—a personal experience of the poet's, not a flight of fancy:

> 'Now, entering, thou shalt haply seated see
> Besides his spouse, his infants on his knee;

Or, turning page by page with studious look
Some bulky paper or God's holy Book.'

Good times came to Dr. Young. The seed he had sown bore fruit. For awhile England had woke up to attack the Stuart doctrine of royal prerogative in Church and State. The men of Suffolk had been the foremost in the fight, and in 1643 we find the Doctor in Duke's Place, London. A sermon was preached by him before p. 295the House of Commons, and printed by order of the House. A Stowmarket Rector speaks of it naturally as a very prolix, learned, somewhat dull and heavy effort to encourage them to persevere in their civil war against the King; but he has the grace to add: 'There is much less of faction in it than many others, and it is rather the production of a contemplative than of an active partisan.' 'One of his examples,' writes Mr. Hollingsworth, 'is from 2 Sam. xiii. 28, where the command of Absalom was to kill Amnon: "Could the command of a *mortal man* infuse that courage and valour into the hearts *of his servants* as to make them adventure upon a *desperate* design? And shall not the command of the *Almighty God* raise up the hearts of His people employed by Him in any work to which *He* calls them, raise up their hearts in following at His command!"' The Doctor had not cleared himself of all the errors of his times. He urged on his hearers, by the example of the Emperors, the necessity of maintaining the doctrine of the Trinity uncorrupt, by the aid of the civil power. He urged, however, on them personal holiness, in order that the reformation of the Church might be more easily accomplished. The two legislative enactments he wished them to pass p. 296were to confer a power upon the Presbyterian clergy to exclude men from the Sacrament, and enforce a better observance of the Sabbath-day. The sermon is scarce, but is bound up with others in the Library at Cambridge, preached at the monthly fasts before the House of Commons.

In the library of the Memorial Hall, Farringdon Street, where assuredly the portrait of the Stowmarket Rector should find a place, there is a copy of this sermon, which was preached at the last solemn fast. February 28, 1643, with the notice that 'It is this day ordered by the Commoners' House of Parliament that Sir John Trevor and Mr. Rous do from this House give thanks to Mr. Young for the great paines hee tooke in the sermon hee preached that day at the intreaty of the said House of Commons at St. Margaret's, Westminster, it being the day of publike humiliation, and to desire him to print this sermon;' which accordingly was done, under the title of 'Hope's Encouragement.' The motto on the outside was: 'Which hope we have as an anchor of the soul both sure and steadfast, and entereth into that which is within the veil.' The sermon was printed in London for Ralph Smith, at the sign of the Bible, in Cornhill, near the Royal Exchange. In p. 297his sermon the preacher took for his text: 'Be of good courage, and He shall strengthen your heart, all ye that wait upon the Lord.' The three propositions established are: First, that God's people are taught by the Lord in all their troubles to wait patiently on Him. The second is that such as wait patiently upon the Lord must rouse themselves with strength and courage to further wait upon Him; and that, thirdly, when God's people wait upon Him, He will increase their courage. The preacher quotes the Hebrew and Augustine, and reasons in a most undeniable manner in support of his propositions; but above all things he is practical. 'The work you are now called on to do,' he says to the M.P.'s, 'is a work of great concernment. It is the purging of the Lord's floor. As it hath reference both to the Church and the Commonwealth, a work sure enough to be encountered with great opposition. Yet I must say it is a work with the managing whereof God hath not so honoured others which have gone before you in your places, but hath reserved it to make you the instruments of His glory in advancing it, and that doth much add unto your honour. Was it an honour to the Tyrians that they were counted amongst the builders of the Temple when Hiram sent to p. 298Solomon things necessary for that work? How, then, hath God honoured you, reserving to you the care of re-edifying His Church (the throne of the living God) and the repairing of the shattered Commonwealth, so far borne down before He raised you to support it, that succeeding ages may with honour to your names, say, "This was the Reforming Parliament," a work which God, by His blessing on your unwearied pains, hath much furthered already, whilst He, by you, hath removed the rubbish that might hinder the raising up of that godly structure appointed and prescribed by the Lord in His Word.' They were to stick to the truth, contended the preacher, quoting the edict of the Emperor Justinian in the Arian controversy, and the reply of Basil the Great to the Emperor's deputy: 'That none trained up in

Holy Scriptures would suffer one syllable of Divine truth to be betrayed; but were ready, if it be required, to suffer any death in the defence thereof.' People, he maintained, are ever carried on by the example of their governors. 'How,' he asks, 'was the Eastern Empire polluted with execrable Arianism, whilst yet the Western continued in the truth? The historians give the reason of it. Constantine, an Arian, ruled in the East when at the same time p. 299Constans and Constantius, sons to Constantine the Great, treading in the steps of their pious father, adhered to the truth professed by him, and so did as far ennoble the Western Empire with the truth as the other did defile the Eastern with his countenancing of error and heresy.' The preacher here asks his hearers to make no laws against religion and piety, and 'recall such as have been made in time of ignorance against the same, and study to uphold and maintain such profitable and wholesome laws as have been formerly enacted for God and His people. Improve what was well begun by others before you, and not perfected by them.' Under this latter head he dwelt on the possible abuse of the Holy Sacrament of the Lord's Supper, and the irreligious profanation of the Lord's Day.

In 1643 the Earl of Manchester ejected many of the Royalist clergymen from their livings who were scandalous ministers. Dr. Sterne having been deprived of the mastership of Jesus College, Cambridge, the Stowmarket Vicar was placed there in his stead. He held the situation till 1654, when, on his refusal of the engagement, Government deprived him of his office. At the time the sermon was preached Dr. Young was one of the far-famed p. 300Assembly of Divines which met in Henry VII.'s chapel in accordance with the Solemn League and Covenant, which proposed three grand objects: 'To endeavour the extirpation of Popery, Prelacy superstition, heresy, and profaneness; to endeavour the preservation of the reformed religion in Scotland and the reformation of religion in the kingdoms of England and Ireland in doctrine, worship, discipline, and government according to the Word of God and the example of the best Reformed Church; and to endeavour to bring the Churches of God in the three kingdoms to the nearest conjunction and uniformity in religion—confession of faith, form of Church government, directory for worship and catechizing; that we and our posterity after us may as brethren live in faith and love, and that the Lord may delight to dwell in the midst of us.' A clause was inserted to the effect that it was English prelacy which they contemned; and thus modified, after all due solemnities, and with their right hands lifted to heaven, was the Solemn League and Covenant sworn to by the English Parliament and by the Assembly of Divines in St. Margaret's Church, September 25, 1643. It was, writes a Presbyterian divine, too much the creature of the Long Parliament who convoked the meeting, p. 301selected the members of Assembly, nominated its president, prescribed its bye-laws, and kept a firm hold and a vigilant eye on all their proceedings. Still, with all these drawbacks, it must be admitted that Parliament could hardly have made a selection of more pious, learned, and conscientious men. The Assembly consisted of men nominated by the members for each county sending in suitable names. The two divines appointed for Suffolk were Mr. Thomas Young, of Stowmarket, and Mr. John Phillips, of Rentall. The Vicar, it is said, sometimes acted as chairman, but this, as Mr. Hollingsworth remarks, is doubtful.

Mr. Young's claim to fame rests on something greater than his sermon, or his position in the Assembly of Divines at Westminster, or his mastership of Jesus College. He was, as we have said, Milton's schoolmaster. The poet tells us:

> ''Tis education forms the common mind;
> Just as a twig is bent the tree's inclined.'

If so, much of Milton's piety and lofty principle and massive learning must have come to him from the Stowmarket Vicar. In our day there is little chance of a young scholar becoming imbued with Miltonian ideas on the subject of civil and religious p. 302liberty. That sublime genius which was to sing in immortal verse of

> 'Man's first disobedience, and the fruit
> Of that forbidden tree, whose mortal taste
> Brought death into the world, and all our woe,'

must have owed much to Dr. Young—a debt which the poet acknowledged, as we have already seen, in no niggardly way. Amongst Milton's Latin letters is the following, which has been translated by Professor Masson thus: 'Although I had resolved with myself, most excellent preceptor, to send you a certain small epistle composed in metrical numbers, yet I did not consider that I had done enough unless I also wrote something in prose: for, truly, the singular and boundless gratitude of my mind which your deserts justly claim from me was not to be expressed in that cramped mode of speech, straitened by fixed feet and syllables, but in a free oration—nay, rather, if it were possible, in an Asiatic exuberance of words. To express sufficiently how much I owe you, were a work far greater than my strength, even if I should call into play all those commonplaces of argument which Aristotle or that dialectician of Paris (Ramus) has collected, or even if I should exhaust all the fountains of oratory. You complain p. 303as justly that my letters have been to you very few and very short; but I, on the other hand, do not so much grieve that I have been remiss in a duty so pleasant and so enviable, as I rejoice, and all but exult, at having such a place in your friendship, as that you should care to ask for frequent letters from me. That I should never have written to you for over more than three years, I pray you will not misconceive, but, in accordance with your wonderful indulgence and candour, put the more charitable construction on it; for I call God to witness how much, as a father, I regard you, with what singular devotion I have always followed you in thought, and how I feared to trouble you with my writings. In sooth, I make it my first care, that since there is nothing else to commend my letters, that their rarity may commend them. Next, as out of that most vehement desire after you which I feel, I always fancy you with me, and speak to you, and beheld you as if you were present, and so, as always happens in love, soothe my grief by a certain vain imagination of your presence, it is, in truth, my fear, as soon as I meditate sending you a letter, that it should suddenly come into my mind by what an interval of earth you are distant from me, and so the grief of your absence, already p. 304nearly lulled, should grow fresh and break up my sweet dream. The Hebrew Bible, your truly most acceptable gift, I have already received. These lines I have written in London, in the midst of town distractions, not, as usual, surrounded by books; if, therefore, anything in this epistle should please you less than might be, and disappoint your expectations, it will be made up for by another more elaborate one as soon as I have returned to the haunts of the Muses.'

When the above letter was written, Milton had become a Cambridge student, where he was to experience a new kind of tutor.

Milton could not get on with Chappell as he did with Young. The tie between the Stowmarket Vicar and the poet was of a much more cordial character.

Again the poet appears to have forwarded the following letter to the Stowmarket Vicarage. It is to be feared that few such precious epistles find their way there now. Milton writes to the Doctor: 'On looking at your letter, most excellent preceptor, this alone struck me as superfluous, that you excused your slowness in writing; for though nothing could come to me more desirable than your letters, how could I or ought I to hope that you should have so much leisure from serious and p. 305more sacred affairs, especially as that is a matter entirely of kindness, and not at all of duty? That, however, I should suspect that you had forgotten me, your so many recent kindnesses to me would by no means allow. I do not see how you could dismiss out of your memory one laden with so great benefits by you. Having been invited by you to your part of the country, as soon as spring has a little advanced I will gladly come to enjoy the delights of the year, and not less of your conversation, and will then withdraw myself from the din of town to your Stoa of the Iceni, as to that most celebrated porch of Zeno or the Tusculan Villa of Cicero, where you with moderate means, but regal spirit, like some Serranus or Curius, placidly reign in your little farm, and contemning fortune, hold as it were a triumph over riches, ambition, pomp, luxury, and whatever the herd of man admire and are amazed by. But as you have deprecated the blame of slowness, you will also, I hope, pardon me the fault of haste; for having put off this letter, I preferred writing little, and that rather in a slovenly manner, to not writing at all. Farewell, much-to-be respected Sir.'

The question is, Did Milton carry out this intention, and pay Stowmarket a visit? Professor p. 306Masson thinks he may have been there in the memorable summer and autumn of 1630. The Rev. Mr. Hollingsworth, the Stowmarket historian argues that it is not unlikely that several, if not many, visits, extending over a period of thirty years, while the tutor held the living, were made by the poet to the place. Tradition has constantly associated his name with the mulberry-trees of the Vicarage, which he planted, but of these only one remains. 'This venerable relic of the past,' continues the Vicar, 'is much decayed, and is still in vigorous bearing. Its girth, before it breaks into branches, is ten feet, and I have had in one season as much as ten gallons from the pure juices of its fruits, which yields a highly flavoured and brilliant-coloured wine.' It stands a few yards distant from the oldest part of the house, and opposite the windows of an upstair double room, which was formerly the sitting-parlour of the Vicar, and where, it is to be believed, the poet and his friend had many a talk of the way to advance religion and liberty in the land, to remove hirelings out of the Church, and to abolish the Bishops. There too, perhaps, might have come to the guest visions of 'Paradise Lost.' In his first work Milton throws out something like a hint of the great p. 307poem which he was in time to write. 'Then, amidst,' to quote his own sonorous language, 'the hymns and hallelujahs of saints, *someone* may, perhaps, be heard offering in high strains, in new and lofty measures, to sing and celebrate Thy Divine mercies and marvellous judgments in this land throughout all ages.' We can easily believe how, in the Stowmarket Vicarage, the plan of the poet may have been talked over, and the heart of the poet encouraged to the work. Regarding Young as Milton did, we may be sure that he would have been only too glad to listen to his suggestions and adopt his advice. There must have been a good deal of plain living and high thinking at the Stowmarket Vicarage when Milton came there as an occasional guest. This is the more probable as Milton's earliest publications were in support of the views of Smectymnian divines. His friendship for Young probably led him into the field of controversy, for he owns that he was not disposed to this manner of writing 'wherein, knowing myself inferior to myself, led by the genial power of nature to another task, I have the use, as I may account, but of my left hand.' It is a fact that Milton was thus drawn into the controversy, and what more natural than that he should have been p. 308induced to do so by the Stowmarket Vicar in the Stowmarket Vicarage? The poet's family were familiar with that part of Suffolk, and his brother, Sir Christopher, who was a stanch Royalist and barrister, lived at Ipswich, but twelve miles off. He went to see Milton, and Milton might have visited Ipswich and Stowmarket at the same time. Be that as it may, tradition and probability alike justify the belief that Milton came to Stowmarket, and that he went away all the wiser and better, all the stronger to do good work for man and God, for his age and all succeeding ages. Young, as it may be inferred, was held in high honour by his friends. He was spoken of by two neighbouring ejected Rectors as the reverend, learned, orthodox, prudent, and holy Dr. Young. When he died, an epitaph was inscribed with some care by a friendly hand, and an unwilling admission is made of the opposition he had encountered. It is now illegible, and some of its lines appear to have been carefully erased — by some High Church chisel, probably. But the following copy was made when the epitaph was fresh and legible:

> 'Here is committed to earth's trust
> Wise, pious, spotlesse, learned dust,
> Who living more adorned the place
> Than the place him. Such was God's grace.'

p. 309Is the verse of this epitaph from Milton's pen or not? Mr. Hollingsworth writes: 'The probability is quite in favour that the pupil should write the last memorial of one whom he so highly honoured and loved as his old master. Nor is the verse itself, with the exception of the last line, unlike the character of Milton's poetry, and this last may have been mutilated and rendered inharmonious by the action of the stone-cutter, who also confused the death of the father and son.' It is pleasant to think, not only that Milton now and then came to the Stowmarket Vicarage, but that in the church itself there is a slight record of his poetical fame. Let me add, as a further illustration of the connection of the great poet with the county of Suffolk, that I am informed one of the family of the Meadowses, of Witnesham, was for a time one of his secretaries.

Young died, aged sixty-eight, in the year 1655, when Milton was fully embarked in public life, when he could spare but little time; but we may be sure that he would be the last at that time of life to forget all that he owed to his tutor Young. Wife and son had predeceased the Vicar. It seems as if there was no one left but the poet to record on the marble in the middle aisle, in front p. 310of the present reading-desk, the virtues of a character which had long exercised so beneficial an influence on his own, and which he had loved so well. Milton's regret for the loss of such a guide, philosopher, and friend must have been lasting and sincere.

p. 311CHAPTER XI.
in constable's county.

East Bergholt—The Valley of the Stour—Painting from nature—East Anglian girls.

Charles Kingsley was wont to glorify the teaching of the hills, and to maintain that the man of the mountain is more imaginative and poetical than the man of the plain. There are many Scotch people, mostly those born in the Highlands, who tell us much the same. If the theory be true—and I am not aware that it is—the exceptions are striking and many. Lincolnshire is rather a flat country, but it gave us (I can never bring myself to call him Lord) Alfred Tennyson. Many of our greatest poets and artists were cockneys; and Constable, that sweet painter of cornfields and shady lanes and quiet rivers, used to say that the scenes of his boyhood made him a painter. I was one autumn in Constable's county, and I do not wonder at it. It is a wonderful district. I p. 312trod all the while, it seemed to me, on enchanted ground: in the gilded mist of autumn, with its river and its marsh lands, where the cows lazily fed—or got under the pollards to be out of the way of the flies—where laughing children swarmed along the hedges in pursuit of the ripe blackberry, where every cottage front was a thing of beauty, with its ivy creeping up the roof or over the wall; while the little garden was a mass of flowers. We expected to see the old gods and goddesses again to participate in the joyousness of an ancient mirth.

Nor was it altogether a flat land, sacred to fat cattle and wheat and turnips. All round me were the elements of romance. At one end of the Vale of Dedham is a hill whence you may look all along the valley (Constable has made it the subject of one of his pictures) as far as Harwich; and as I lingered by the Stour—the river which divides Essex and Suffolk—East Bergholt, clothed with woods and crowned with a church, in which there is a stained-glass window put up in honour of Constable, and a baptismal font, the gift of Constable's brother, unfolded to my wondering eye all her rural charms. There are people who love to climb hills; I hate to do so. It is all vanity and p. 313vexation of spirit; when you get to the top of one hill the chances are all you see is another hill, to the top of which you will have to climb. Give me a country lane, with its luxuriant hedges, its shady trees, its flowers, its richness of greensward, its pigs and poultry and farmyard; there is poetry in such nooks and corners of the earth, as Burns and Bloomfield and Gerald Massey found. No wonder the place made Constable an artist, and an artist whose name will not speedily pass away. My dear sir or madam, the next time you are on your way from London to Ipswich, don't rush along at express speed; get out at Ardleigh, make your way to the Vale of Dedham, then walk along the Stour, and cross it by a couple of rustic bridges, and you are at East Bergholt, in Suffolk, where Constable was born, and if you do so you will bless me evermore. Then, if you like, rejoin the train at Manningtree, and resume your journey. Few East Anglians even are aware of the wealth of beauty in that quiet corner. 'The beauty of the surrounding scenery,' writes Constable's biographer, 'its gentle declivities, its luxuriant meadows, flats sprinkled with flocks and herds, its well-cultivated Uplands, its woods and rivers, with mansions scattered, and churches, farms, and picturesque p. 314cottages—all impart to this spot an amenity and elegance hardly anywhere else to be found.'

The Constables have been long in the district. The grandfather was a farmer at a village close by. The father, who was well-to-do, purchased a water-mill at Dedham and two windmills at East Bergholt, where he lived. The great artist, his son John, was born in the last century, and was educated at Lavenham and the Dedham Grammar School, and when the lad had reached sixteen or seventeen became addicted to painting, his studio being in the house of a Mr. John Dunthorne, a painter and glazier, with whom he remained on terms of the greatest intimacy for many years. The father would fain have made the son a farmer. He preferred to be a miller, and in his young days was known in the district as the handsome miller. His windmills, when he took to painting, were wonderful, and well deserved the criticism of his brother, who used to say, 'When I look at a windmill painted by John, I see that it will go round, which is not always the case with those of other artists,' for the simple reason that John knew what he was about, which the others did not. Again, his industrial career helped him in another way. A miller learns to study the clouds, and Constable's p. 315clouds were exceptionally life-like and real. The handsome young miller soon acquired artistic friends, one of them being Sir George Beaumont, the guide, philosopher, and friend of most of the geniuses of that time. Said another to him, 'Do not trouble yourself about inventing figures for a landscape; you cannot remain an hour in a spot without the appearance of some living thing, that will in all probability better accord with the scene and the time of day than any invention of your own.' After a visit to his artist friends in London, he resumed his mill life, and in 1779 he finally commenced his artistic career, and painted all the country round. His studies were chiefly Dedham, East Bergholt, the Valley of the Stour, and the neighbouring village of Stratford. At Stoke Nayland he painted an altar-piece for the church. There is also another altar-piece in a neighbouring church, but his altar-pieces are not known or treasured like his other works.

Cooper tells a good story of Constable. One day Stodart, the sculptor, met Fuseli starting forth with an old umbrella. 'Why do you carry the umbrella?' asked the sculptor. 'I am going to see Constable,' was the reply, 'and he is always painting rain.' One can only remark that, if p. 316Constable was always painting rain, he always did it well.

Another good story was told Redgrave by Lee. 'I hear you sell all your pictures,' said Constable to the younger landscape-painter. 'Why, yes,' said Lee; 'I'm pretty fortunate. Don't you sell yours?' 'No,' said Constable, 'I don't sell any of my pictures, and I'll tell you why: when I paint a *bad* picture I don't like to part with it, and when I paint a *good* one I like to keep it.' It is well known that one year when Constable was on the Council of the Royal Academy, one of his own pictures was passed by mistake before the judges. 'Cross it,' said one. 'It won't do,' said another. 'Pass on,' said a third. And the carpenter was just about to chalk it with a cross, when he read the name of 'John Constable.' Of course there were lame apologies, and the picture was taken from the condemned heap and placed with the works of his brother Academicians. But after work was over Constable took the picture under his arm, and, despite the remonstrance of his brother colleagues, marched off with it, saving: 'I can't think of its being hung after it has been fairly turned out. The work so condemned was the 'Stream bordered in with Willows,' now in the South Kensington p. 317Museum. Leslie once remarked to Redgrave that he would give any work he had painted for it, so warmly did he admire it.

'Constable is the best landscape-painter we have,' wrote Frith to his mother in 1835. 'He is a very merry fellow, and very rich. He told us an anecdote of a man who came to look at his pictures; he was a gardener. One day he called him into his painting-room to look at his pictures, when the man made the usual vulgar remarks, such as, "Did you do all this, sir?" "Yes." "What, all this?" "Yes." "What, frame and all?" At last he came to an empty frame that was hung against the wall without any picture in it, when he said to Constable, "But you don't call this picture quite finished, do you, sir?" Constable said that quite sickened him, and he never let any ignoramuses ever see his pictures again, or frames either.'

Constable's great merits, writes Mr. Frith, were first recognised in France, with the result upon French landscape art that is felt at the present time. His advice to Frith was: 'Never do anything without nature before you if it be possible to have it. See those weeds and the dock leaves? They are to come into the foreground of this p. 318picture. I know dock leaves pretty well, but I should not attempt to introduce them into a picture without having them before me.'

Constable died very suddenly in 1837. His fame, now that he is dead, is greater than when he was alive. His work abides in all its strength.

There is little in East Bergholt to remind one of Constable, where his reputation remains as that of a genial and kindly-hearted man; but the landscape in all its essential features remains the same. The house in which he was born was pulled down in 1841, which is a great pity, as it is described as a large and handsome mansion. But I never saw a small village with so many attractive residences, though why anybody should live in any of them I could not, for the life of me, understand. Yet there they were, quite a street of them, all in beautiful order, as if they were the residences of wealthy citizens in the suburbs of a busy town. They ought to have been filled with handsome girls, as Charles Kingsley tells us East Anglia is famed for the beauty of its women; all I can say, however, is that I saw none of them, or any sign of life anywhere, beyond the inevitable tradesmen's carts. Independently of Constable, East Bergholt claims to be worth a pilgrimage for its rustic beauty, p. 319which, however, becomes tame and common as you get away from it. The church is old, and has a history — of little consequence, however, to anyone now. One of its rectors was burned at Ipswich in Queen Mary's reign. His name, Samuel, ought to be preserved by a Church which, till lately, had few martyrs of its own. East Bergholt has also a Congregational and Primitive Methodist chapel, and a colony of Benedictine nuns, driven away from France by the great Revolution. We are a hospitable people, and we are proud to be so, but have we not just at this time too many refugee nuns and monks in our midst?

p. 320CHAPTER XII.
east anglian worthies.

Suffolk cheese — Danes, Saxons, and Normans — Philosophers and statesmen — Artists and literati.

Abbo Floriacencis, who flourished in the year a.d. 910, describes East Anglia as 'very noble, and particularly because of its being watered on all sides. On the south and east it is encompassed by the ocean, on the north by the moisture of large and wet fens which, arising almost in the heart of the island, because of the evenness of the ground for a hundred miles and more, descend in great rivers into the sea. On the west the province is joyned to the rest of the island, and, therefore, may be entered (by land); but lest it should be harassed by the frequent incursions of the enemy it is fortifyed with an earthen rampire like a high wall, and with a ditch. The inner parts of it is a pretty rich soil, made exceeding pleasant by gardens and groves, rendered agreeable by its p. 321convenience for hunting, famous for pasturage, and abounding with sheep and all sorts of cattle. I do not insist upon its rivers full of fish, considering that a tongue as it were of the sea itself licks it on one side, and on the other side the large fens make a prodigious number of lakes two or three miles over. These fens accommodate great numbers of monks with their desired retirement and solitude, with which, being enclosed, they have no occasion for the privacy of a wilderness.' Before the monks came the place was held by the Iceni — a stout and valiant people, as Tacitus describes them. In the time of the Heptarchy, King Uffa was their lord and master. In later times Suffolk, when explored by Camden, was celebrated for its cheeses, which, to the great advantage of the inhabitants, were bought up through all England, nay, in Germany also, with France and Spain, as Pantaleon Medicus has told us, who scruples not to set them against those of Placentia both in colour and taste. To the Norfolk people, it must be admitted, Camden gives the palm. The goodness of the soil of that country, he argues, 'may be gathered from hence, that the inhabitants are of a bright, clear complexion, not to mention their sharpness of wit and admirable quickness in the p. 322study of our common law. So that it is at present, and always has been, reputed the common nursery of lawyers, and even amongst the common people you shall meet with a great many who (as one expresses it), if they have no just quarrel, are able to raise it out of the very quirks and niceties of the law.' In our time it is rather the fashion to run down the East Anglians, yet that they have done their duty to their country no one can deny. 'They say we are Norfolk fules,' said a waiter at a Norfolk hotel, to me, a little while ago; 'but I ain't ashamed of my county, for all that.' Why should he be, the reader naturally asks?

The Saxons of East Anglia gave the name of England to this land of ours; but before this time East Anglia had attained, by means of its sons and daughters, to fame far and near. If we may believe Gildas, a Christian church was planted in England in the time of Nero. Claudia, to whom Paul refers in Philippians and Timothy, was a British lady of great wit and greater beauty, celebrated by the poet Martial. She may have been converted by Paul, argued the Rev. Mr. Hollingsworth, a local historian, Rural Dean and Rector of Stowmarket; nor is it at all improbable, he adds, 'that Claudia, the British beauty, may have been p. 323an Iceni, or East Anglian lady, as her brilliant complexion, for which so many in these counties are celebrated, had caused a vivid feeling of sensation and curiosity and envy even among the haughty dames of the imperial city of Rome.' The Romans were glad to make terms with the Iceni till the unfortunate Boadicea perished in the revolt which she had so rashly raised. The Saxons came after the Romans, and took possession of the land. Saxon proprietors compelled the people, whose lives they spared, to till the very lands on which their fathers had lived under the Roman Government or their own chiefs. Pagan worship was reintroduced; but when Sigberht, the son of Redwald, King of East Anglia, reigned, he sent to France for Christian ministers, and one of them, Felix, a Burgundian, landed at Felixstowe, and there commenced his Christian labours. Felix was held in high repute by the Bishops in other parts of the kingdom. His opinions were quoted and revered. The diocese was large, and the fourth Bishop divided it into two parts, the second Bishop being planted at North Elmham, in Norfolk. In 955 the see was again united, when Erfastus, the twenty-second Bishop, removed to Thetford. A little while after the Bishop's residence was removed p. 324to Norwich, and there it has ever since remained; but the land was not long permitted to remain in peace. In 870 a large party of Danes marched from Lincolnshire into Suffolk, defeated King Edmund, near Hoxne, and, as he would not become an idolater, shot him to death with arrows. Bury St. Edmunds still preserves the name and fame of one of the most illustrious of our Anglo-Saxon martyrs. King Alfred, with a policy worthy of his sagacity, made Guthrum, the Danish governor of Suffolk, a Christian, and continued him in his rule. The Danes in East Anglia were then an immense army, and thus at once they were turned from foes into friends. Guthrum was baptized, and it is to be hoped was all the better for it. At any rate, he returned to Suffolk and divided many of the estates which had been held by Saxon proprietors killed in war. He died in peace, and had a fitting funeral at Hadleigh. The children of those Danish soldiers were dangerous friends, and too frequently betrayed the Saxons. Blood is thicker than water, and as each succeeding band of Danish adventurers landed on our eastern coast, they were welcomed by such followers of Guthrum as had settled in Suffolk as friends and allies. Nevertheless, the Danes found the conquest p. 325of the island impossible. Divine Providence, Mr. Hollingsworth tells us, did not suffer the Saxon race to be vanquished by those who were connected with them by blood. Nevertheless, the struggle was long and severe. The two races were equally matched in courage, but the Saxon surpassed his foe in that stern, unyielding endurance which enabled him to resist every defeat and prepare again for the contest. The whole surface of the country became studded with entrenchments, moats, and mounds, within whose line the harassed Saxon defended his property and all he valued in his home. History begins, as far as England is practically concerned, with the Norman Conquest. It was then the Norsemen, blue-eyed, fair-haired, the finest blood in Europe, planted themselves in Norfolk and Suffolk, and brought with them feudalism and civilization. It was in 787 that, according to the Saxon Chronicle, they first reached England; but it was not till William the Conqueror made the land his own that they settled as English lords, and divided between them the land in which their rapacious forefathers had won many a precious treasure.

'The red gold and the white silver
He covets as a leech does blood,'

wrote an old poet of the Norseman.

p. 326Let us take, as an illustration of the county, a Norfolk family. In Westminster Abbey there is monument to Sir Thomas Fowell Buxton, who was buried in the ruined chancel of the little church at Overstrand, near Northrepps, 'a droll, irregular, unconventional-looking place,' as Caroline Fox calls it, where he loved at all times to live, and where he retired to die. The family from which Sir Thomas descended resided, about the middle of the sixteenth century, at Sudbury, in Suffolk. It was while at Earlham that he made his dibut as a public speaker at one of the earlier meetings of the Norfolk Bible Society. In the winter of 1817 he went over to France with some of the Gurneys and the Rev. Francis Cunningham, who was anxious to establish a Bible Society in Paris. He was also anxious to inquire into the way in which the gaols at Antwerp and Ghent were conducted. On his return he examined minutely into the state of the London gaols, and, to use his own expression, his inquiries developed a system of folly and wickedness which surpassed belief. In the following year he published a work entitled 'An Inquiry whether Crime be Produced or Prevented by our Present System of Penal Discipline,' which ran through six editions, and tended powerfully to create a proper p. 327public feeling on the subject. In 1819 we find him in Parliament seconding Sir James Mackintosh in his efforts to promote a reform of our criminal law — then the most sanguinary in Europe. One of his earliest efforts was to get the House to abolish the burning of widows in India; and in 1821 he received from Wilberforce the command to relieve him of a responsibility too heavy for his advancing years and infirmities — the care of the slave: a holy enterprise for which Mr. Buxton had been qualifying himself by careful thought and study, and which he was spared to carry to a successful end. At first he resided at Cromer Hall, an old seat of the Windham family, which no longer exists, having been pulled down and replaced by a modern residence. It was situated about a quarter of a mile from the sea, but sheltered from the north winds by closely surrounding hills and woods, and with its old buttresses, gables, and porches clothed with roses and jessamine, and its famed lawn, where the pheasants came down to feed, had a peculiar character of picturesque simplicity. The interior corresponded with its external appearance, and had little of the regularity of modern building. One attic chamber was walled up, with no entrance save through the window: and at different times p. 328large pits were discovered under the floor or in the thick walls—used, it was supposed, in old times by the smugglers of the coast. There is much picturesque scenery around Cromer, and large parties were often made up for excursions to Sherringham—one of the most beautiful spots in all the eastern counties, to the wooded dells of Felbrigg and Runton, or to the rough heath ground by the beach beacon. One who was a frequent guest at Cromer Hall wrote: 'I wish I could describe the impression made upon me by the extraordinary power of interesting and stimulating others which was possessed by Sir Fowell Buxton some thirty years ago. In my own case it was like having powers of thinking, powers of feeling, and, above all, the love of true poetry suddenly aroused within me, which, though I had possessed them before, had been till then unused. From Locke "On the Human Understanding," to "William of Deloraine, good at need," *he* woke up in me the sleeping principle of taste, and, in giving me such objects of pursuit, has added immeasurably to the happiness of my life.' On a Sunday afternoon, we are told, his large dining-hall was filled with a miscellaneous audience of fishermen and neighbours, as well as of his own household, to whom he would read the p. 329Bible, commenting on it at the same time. Very simple and beautiful seems to us that far-away Norfolk life; except that his hospitalities were more bounded by want of room, his life at Northrepps was much the same as it had been at Cromer Hall. It is one of the pleasures of my life that I have heard Sir Thomas speak. In modern England the influence of the Buxton family and name is yet a power.

Having already alluded to the Windhams and Felbrigg, it remains to say that the last of that illustrious line died in 1810. Felbrigg was purchased by the Windhams as far back as 1461. The public life of Windham, the statesman, may be considered as having commenced in 1783, when he undertook the office of Principal Secretary to Lord Northington, who was appointed Lord Lieutenant of Ireland. The great Marquis of Lansdowne, when he was last at Felbrigg, in 1861, said Mr. Windham had the best Parliamentary address of any man he had ever seen, which was enhanced by the grace of his person and the dignity of his manners. Still more glowing was the testimony borne to Mr. Windham by Earl Grey when he heard of his death.

A mere glance at his diary is sufficient to convince us that Windham, p. 330when in London, mixed with the first men and women of his time. The late Lord Chief Justice Scarlett, on being asked by his son-in-law to name the very best speech he had heard during his life, and that which he thought most worthy of study, answered, without hesitation, 'Windham's speech on the Law of Evidence.' In a conversation with Lord Palmerston, Pitt observed of Windham: 'Nothing can be so well-meaning or eloquent as he is. His speeches are the finest productions possible of warm imagination and fancy.' In 1800 we read in the Malmesbury Diaries that old George III. had meant Windham to be his First Minister. As a friend of Burke and Johnson, Windham's name will not easily fade away. It is to him we owe the most pathetic account of the closing hours of the Monarch of Bolt Court.

Sir Cloudesley Shovel may well claim to be one of Norfolk's heroes. Born in an obscure village, an apprentice to a shoemaker, he obtained rank and fame as one of Queen Anne's most honoured Admirals. It is denied that he was in very humble circumstances, and it is a fact that his original letters were so well worded as to indicate that he had received a fair education. At any rate, he went to sea at ten years old with p. 331his friend Sir John Hadough; and although not a cabin-boy in the modern acceptation of that term, he undertook his captain's errands, swimming on one occasion through the enemy's fire with some despatches for a distant ship, carrying the papers in his mouth, displaying a courage worthy of admiration. He distinguished himself in the Battle of Bantry Bay. As an enemy of France and Spain, he triumphed in many a fierce fight. Returning home flushed with victory, his ship and all on board were lost on the Scilly Isles in an October gale. Some uncertainty hangs over his last moments. It is asserted that he swam to shore alive, and that he was put to death for the sake of his ring of emeralds and diamonds. An ancient woman is stated to have confessed as much. For the honour of human nature, we would fain believe the story to be untrue. A still greater Norfolk hero was Lord Nelson, who is buried in St. Paul's Cathedral. 'My principle,' said Nelson, on one occasion, 'is to assist in driving the French to the devil, and in restoring peace and happiness to mankind.' Whether he succeeded as regards the former we are not in a position to state; but peace and happiness, alas! are still far from being the p. 332common property of mankind. The rectory house at Burnham Thorpe, where Nelson was born, exists no longer. Sir Cloudesley Shovel lived in a castellated stone house in the small agricultural village of Cockthorpe, originally fortified as a defence against the incursions of smugglers. A room in this house, entered by a doorway arched over with stone, is shown, which is still called by the villagers Sir Cloudesley's drawing-room.

A chapter might be written about the Norfolk Cokes. Sir Edward Coke, the great lawyer, was buried at Tittleshale, in Norfolk. The well-known Coke, the distinguished agriculturist, inhabited that splendid Holkham, the fame of which exists in our day. It was begun by Lord Leicester in 1734, and finished by his Countess in 1764. Blomefield, the well-known Norfolk historian, speaks of it as a noble, stately, and sumptuous palace. Lord Coke and Lord Burlington were men of similar tastes and pursuits, and were diligent students of classical and Italian art. The Holkham Library still contains treasures rich and rare. Many of the latter formed part of the library of Sir Edward Coke; the title-page of the first edition of the 'Novum Organum,' published in 1620, bears the design of a ship passing through p. 333the Pillars of Hercules into an undulating sea. The Holkham copy is adorned by the inscription, 'Ex dono auctoris.'

Above the ship, in the handwriting of Coke, is the couplet:

'It deserveth not to be read in schools,
But to be freighted in the ship of fools.'

Thomas Shadwell, the Poet Laureate and historiographer of William III., was a Norfolk man. He is buried in Westminster Abbey. It is said by Noble that he was an honest man. Of course he was. Chalmers accuses him of indecent conversation, or Lord Rochester would not have said that he had more wit and humour than any other poet. I am afraid he confers little honour on his native county. 'Others,' wrote Dryden in one of his satires,

'To some faint meaning make pretence,
But Shadwell never deviates into sense.'

Sir Robert Walpole, who saved England from wooden shoes and slavery, was of a Norfolk family, yet flourishing; as are the Townshends, to whom we owe the introduction of the turnip. Norfolk also can boast of Sir Thomas Gresham and Sir Francis Walsingham. In Norfolk was born that 'great oracle of law, patron of the Church, and p. 334glory of England,' as Camden calls him, Sir Henry Spelman. At Bickling, in the same county, was born that ill-starred Anne Boleyn, of whom it is written that

> 'Love could teach a monarch to be wise,
> And Gospel light first beamed from Boleyn's eyes.'

In the same neighbourhood, also, was born John Baconthorpe, the resolute doctor, of whom Pantias Pansa has written: 'This one resolute doctor has furnished the Christian religion with armour against the Jews stronger than that of Vulcan.' Pansa was a Norfolk man, and so was the great botanist Sir W. Hooker.

Who has not heard of Lynn, in Norfolk, where, when Eugene Aram was the usher,

> 'Four-and-twenty happy boys
> Came bounding out of school'?

It was in that old town Fanny Burney, the friend of Mrs. Thrale and Dr. Johnson, the author of novels like 'Evelina,' which people even read nowadays, was born on the 13th of June, 1752. She grew up low of stature, of a brown complexion. One of her friends called her the dove, which she thought was from the colour of her eyes—a greenish-gray; her last editor thinks it must have p. 335been from their kind expression. She was very short-sighted, like her father. In her portrait, taken at the age of thirty, merriment seems latent behind a demure look. At any rate, her countenance was what might be called a speaking one. 'Poor Fanny!' said her father, 'her face tells what she thinks, whether she will or no. I long to see her honest face once more.' 'Poor Fanny' lived to a good old age, and her gossiping diary is a mine of wealth as regards the Royal Family, and Johnson, and Mrs. Thrale, and the cleverest men and women of her time.

Thomas Bilney, one of our Protestant martyrs, was a Norfolk man. It was a Norfolk knight, Sir Thomas Erpingham, who gave signal for the archers at Agincourt. Shakespeare refers to him in his 'King Henry V.' as follows:

'King. — Good-morrow, old Sir Thomas Erping-
ham;
A good soft pillow for that good white head
Were better than a churlish turf of France.
'Erp. — Not so, my liege; this lodging likes me bet-
ter,
Since I may say, now lie I like a king.'

Many East Anglians helped to win the battle of Agincourt. The Earl of Kimberley still bears Agincourt on his shield.

Let us now pass over into Suffolk. It is worth p. 336asking how Suffolk came to earn the nickname of Silly Suffolk. 'Silly,' say the learned, is derived from the German *selig*, meaning 'holy or blessed,' and is said to have been applied to Suffolk on account of the number of beautiful churches it contains; Suffolk, at any rate, is silly no longer. In the present day it shows to advantage, if we may judge by the enterprise and public spirit of such a town as Ipswich, for instance. Not long since, as I landed on the docks at Hamburg, I had the pleasure of seeing some dozen or more steam ploughs and agricultural implements waiting to be transported into the interior. The ploughs and implements bore well-known Suffolk names, such as Garrett and Sons or Ransomes, Sims and Jefferies, and were open manifestations of Suffolk skill and energy, and ability to hold its own against all comers. Amongst the women of the present genera-tion, where are to be met the superiors of Mrs. Garrett Anderson or of Mrs. Fawcett, widow of the distinguished statesman, and mother of a sweet girl-graduate who has beaten all the men at her University? I was the other day at Haverhill, where Mr. D. Gurteen still lives to enjoy, at the ripe old age of eighty-three, the fruits of an energy on his part which has raised p. 337Haverhill from a village of pau-pers into a flourishing community, whose manufactures are to be met with all over the land. One day, as I was walking along Gray's Inn Road, a fine, well-built man stopped me to ask me if I remem-bered him. When he mentioned his name I did directly. He was of the poorest of the poor in his home at Wrentham. He had done well in London. 'You know, sir,' he said, 'how poor our family was. Well, I had enough of poverty, and I made up my mind to come to London and be either a man or a mouse.'

In the London of to-day the heads of some of our greatest establishments are Suffolk men. We all know the stately pile in Holborn, once Meekings', now Wallis's, where all the world and his wife go to buy. Mr. Wallis hails from Stowmarket, and the man who fits up London shops in the most tasty style, Mr. Sage, of Gray's Inn Road, was a Suffolk carpenter, who, when out of work, with his last guinea got some cards printed, one of which got him a job, which ultimately led on to fame and fortune.

No, Suffolk has long ceased to be silly. It must have deserved the title in the days which I can remember when a Conservative M.P., amidst p. 338enthusiastic cheering, at Ipswich, intimated that it was quite as well the sun and moon were placed high up in the heavens, else

'Some reforming ass
Would soon propose to pluck them down
And light the world with gas.'

One of the oddest, most attractive, and most original women of the last century was Elizabeth Simpson, a Suffolk girl, who ran away from her home, where she was never taught anything, at the age of sixteen, to make her fortune, and to win fame. In both cases she succeeded, though not so soon as she could have wished. Failing to touch the hard heart of the manager of the Norwich Theatre, a Welshman of the name of Griffiths, she packed up her things in a bandbox, and, good-looking and audacious, landed herself on the Holborn pavement. 'By the time you receive this,' she wrote to her mother, 'I shall leave Standingfield perhaps for ever. You are surprised, but be not uneasy; believe the step I have undertaken is indiscreet, but by no means criminal, unless I sin by not acquainting you with it. I now endure every pang, am not lost to every feeling, on thus quitting the tenderest and best of parents, I would say most beloved, too, but cannot prove my affection, p. 339yet time may. To that I must submit my hope of retaining your regard. The censures of the world I despise, as the most worthy incur the reproaches of that. Should I ever think you will wish to hear from me I will write.' A pretty, unprotected, unknown girl of sixteen, in London, had, we can well believe, no easy time of it. Strangers followed her in the street, people insulted her in the theatre, suspicious landladies looked her up. Happily, a brother-in-law met her in a penniless state and took her home. Unhappily, at his house she met Inchbald, an indifferent and badly-paid actor. They were immediately married, and the girl rejoiced to think that she was an actress, and about to realize the ambition of her youth. It was no small part which the Suffolk girl felt herself qualified to fill. On the 4th of September, 1772, she made her dibut as Cordelia to her husband's Lear. In 1821 Mrs. Inchbald, famed for her 'simple story,' which took the town by storm, was buried in Kensington Churchyard. But before she got there she had to endure much. At that time theatrical performers were much worse paid than they are now, when, as Mr. Irving tells us, any decent-looking young man, with a good suit of clothes, can command his five p. 340or six pounds a week. Mrs. Inchbald and her husband had to drink of the cup of poverty, and its consequent degradation, to the dregs. On one occasion they took it into their heads to go to France, believing that they could make money—he by painting, she by writing. The scheme, as was to be expected, did not answer, and they were landed on their return somewhere near Brighton, in the September of 1776, literally without a crust of bread. On one occasion it was stated that they dined off raw turnips, stolen from a field as they wandered past. Next year, however, the world began to mend so far as they were concerned.

At Manchester they met the Siddonses and J. P. Kemble, and one result of that meeting was peace and prosperity. At this time also the lady's husband died, and that was no great loss, as the lady was far too independent for a wife. Yet, if the great Kemble had proposed to her, as she used to tell Fanny Kemble, she would have jumped at him. To the last her habits of life were most penurious. She spent nothing on dress, she was indifferent in the matter of eating and drinking, and when she was making as much as from #500 to #900 by a new play, in order to save a trifle she would sit in the depth of p. 341winter without a fire. Only fancy any of our later lady-novelists thus ascetic and self-denying. The idea is absurd. She was to the last what Godwin described her, a mixture of lady and milkmaid. And yet the lady had ambition. She had an idea that she might be Lady Bunbury. However, she marred her chance, at the same time missing a rich Mr. Glover, who offered a marriage settlement of #500 a year. Mrs. Inchbald, however, well knew how to take care of herself. No one better. She had learned the art in rather a hard school, and, besides, she knew how to take care of her poor relations. None of her sisters seem to have done well, and she had to aid them all.

Sudbury was the birthplace of that William Enfield, whose 'Speaker' was the terror and delight of more than one generation of England's ingenuous youth. Lord Chancellor Thurlow, of the rugged eyebrows and the savage look, and fellow-clerk with the poet Cowper, was born at Ashfield, an obscure village not far off. Robert Bloomfield, who wrote the 'Farmer's Boy,' came from Honington, where his mother kept a village school, and where he became a shoemaker. Capel Loft, an amiable gentleman of literary sympathies and pursuits, and Bloomfield's warmest friend, p. 342resided at Troston Hall, in the immediate neighbourhood of Honington. At one time there was no writer better known than John Lydgate, called the Monk of Bury, born at the village of Lydgate, in 1380. 'His language,' writes a learned critic, 'is much less obsolete than Chaucer's, and a great deal more harmonious.' Stephen Gardener, Bishop of Winchester, and an enemy to the Reformation, was born at Bury. At Trinity St. Martin lived Thomas Cavendish, the second Englishman who sailed round the globe. Admiral Broke, memorable for his capture of the *Chesapeake*, when we were at war with America, was born at Nacton. The great non-juring Archbishop Sancroft was born at Fressingfield, where he retired to die, and where he is buried under a handsome monument. The great scholar, Robert Grossetjte, Bishop of Lincoln, was born at Stradbrook. Of him Roger Bacon wrote that he was the only man living who was in possession of all the sciences. Wycliff, on innumerable occasions, refers to him with respect. Arthur Young, the celebrated agriculturist, some of whose sentences are preserved as golden ones — especially that which says, 'Give a man the secure possession of a rock, and he will make a garden of it' — and whose valuable works, I am glad to see, p. 343are republished, was born and lived near Bury St. Edmunds. Echard, the historian, was born at Barsham, in 1671. Porson was a Norfolk lad.

Sir Thomas Hanmer was one of the most independent men that ever sat for the county of Suffolk. Mr. Glyde, of Ipswich, terms him the Gladstone of his age. Pope appears to stigmatize him as a Trimmer,

> 'Courtiers and patrols in two ranks divide;
> Through both he passed, and bowed from side to
> side.'

His garden at Mildenhall was celebrated for the quality of its grapes, and Sir Thomas used to send every year hampers filled with these grapes, and carried on men's shoulders, to London for the Queen. That stubborn Radical and Freethinker, Tom Paine, was born at Thetford. Sir John Suckling, a Suffolk poet, has written, at any rate, one verse never excelled:

> 'Her feet beneath her petticoat,
> Like little mice, stole in and out,
> As if they feared the light.
> But oh, she dances such a way,
> No sun upon an Easter day
> Is half so fine a sight.'

England has in all parts of the world sons and daughters who have deserved well of the State, and not a few of them are East Anglians by birth p. 344and breeding. May their fame be cherished and their examples followed by their successors in that calm, quiet, Eastern land—far from the madding crowd—where the roar and rush of our modern life are almost unknown—where farmers weep and wail but look jolly nevertheless!

the end.

billing and sons, printers, guildford.